Green

W9-BCE-473

16.16

P.O. 69591

Brooks - Cork Library
Shelton State
Community College

DISCARDED

DISCARDED

SHELTON STATE LIBRARY

INTERRACIAL RELATIONSHIPS

Other Books in the At Issue Series:

INTERRACIAL
RELATIONSHIPS

Bryan J. Grapes, *Book Editor*

David L. Bender, *Publisher*
Bruno Leone, *Executive Editor*
Bonnie Szumski, *Editorial Director*
David M. Haugen, *Managing Editor*

An Opposing Viewpoints® Series

Greenhaven Press, Inc.
San Diego, California

No part of this book may be reproduced or used in any form or by any means, electrical, mechanical, or otherwise, including, but not limited to, photocopy, recording, or any information storage and retrieval system, without prior written permission from the publisher.

Library of Congress Cataloging-in-Publication Data

Interracial relationships / Bryan J. Grapes, book editor.
    p.   cm. — (At issue)
    Includes bibliographical references and index.
    ISBN 0-7377-0155-2 (lib. : alk. paper). —
ISBN 0-7377-0154-4 (pbk. : alk. paper)
    1. Intermarriage—United States. 2. Interracial marriage—United States. 3. Ethnicity—United States. 4. United States—Race relations. I. Grapes, Bryan J., 1970– . II. Series: At issue (San Diego, Calif.)
HQ1031.I59   2000
306.84'6—dc21   99-23677
                                                   CIP

©2000 by Greenhaven Press, Inc., PO Box 289009,
San Diego, CA 92198-9009

Printed in the U.S.A.

Every effort has been made to trace owners of copyrighted material.

Table of Contents

Introduction

Interracial romance has been a point of contention in America since the first English settlers established colonies in the seventeenth century. In 1664 Maryland banned interracial marriage due to questions over whether the offspring of a black slave and a white person would be considered a free person or property. In following years, Massachusetts, Pennsylvania, North Carolina, and South Carolina instituted antimiscegenation laws which banned interracial marriage. In 1691 Virginia outlawed interracial couples and labeled their children as "that abominable mixture and spurious issue." When slavery was abolished by the Thirteenth Amendment in 1865, many southern states instituted what were known as the "Black Codes." In addition to stripping freed slaves of most of their newly acquired rights, these codes continued the prohibition of marriage between whites and blacks. This was based on the commonly held notion that Africans, and Native Americans as well, were inferior races and interbreeding would pollute the white gene pool. When Congress tried to override the "Black Codes" by issuing a series of laws from 1866 to 1875, the Supreme Court declared most of the legislation void and upheld the southern states' right to outlaw interracial marriage.

Miscegenation in American history

Antimiscegenation laws did not keep everyone from crossing the color line. Before the Thirteenth Amendment abolished slavery, many white slave masters secretly took advantage of black women, with whom they fathered scores of children. Also, not every state had laws prohibiting interracial marriage. Some estimates indicate that as many as 70 percent of African Americans are descendants of black and white couplings. Famous African Americans such as W.E.B. Du Bois, Booker T. Washington, Malcolm X, Martin Luther King Jr., and Frederick Douglass were of black and white ancestry. Douglass eventually married a white woman, Helen Pitts, after the death of his first wife. Douglass, one of the most vocal African American activists of the Civil War era, felt that intermarriage was the key to the assimilation and acceptance of the newly freed slaves into American society. According to Douglass, "The future of the Negro therefore is . . . that he will be absorbed, assimilated, and it will only appear finally . . . in the features of a blended race."

Not all African Americans wanted to be absorbed however. "We have not asked assimilation; we have resisted it," said W.E.B. Du Bois. "It has been forced on us by brute strength, ignorance, poverty, degradation and fraud." Du Bois also condemned white America's hypocrisy when it came to miscegenation. "It is the white race, roaming the world, that has left its trail of bastards and outraged women and then raised holy hands and deplored 'race mixture.'"

Loving v. Virginia

By the beginning of the civil rights era in the 1950s, antimiscegenation statutes were still on the books in sixteen states, mostly in the South and the Midwest. In 1958 Richard Loving, a white man, and Mildred Jeter, a black woman, went to Washington, D.C., which did not forbid interracial marriage, to get married. When they returned to their Virginia home they were arrested and convicted of violating Virginia's antimiscegenation statute. Under Virginia's law, the 1–5 year prison sentence for marrying across racial lines applied even if the couple was married in a state that allowed interracial marriage. The Lovings were sentenced to one year in prison. For nine years after their arrest they waged a legal battle through the courts, and in 1967 the Supreme Court reversed the Lovings' convictions. "Under our Constitution, the freedom to marry, or not marry, a person of another race resides with the individual and cannot be infringed by the State," wrote Chief Justice Earl Warren in *Loving v. Virginia*. The Supreme Court decision effectively invalidated all existing antimiscegenation legislation.

Increased prevalence of interracial romance

Since the Supreme Court struck down the last of America's antimiscegenation laws, the number of interracial marriages has more than tripled. According to the Census Bureau, the number of mixed-race marriages rose from 300,000 in 1970 to 1.2 million in 1990. Between 1960 and 1990, the percentage of African American marriages involving a white spouse more than tripled. Furthermore, according to recent statistics, 65 percent of Japanese Americans marry outside of their race and 75 percent of Native Americans marry someone of a different ethnic background.

The incidence of interracial dating among American youth has increased even more dramatically. According to some recent studies, as many as 57 percent of teenagers have dated someone outside of their race. An additional 30 percent have indicated that they would consider dating outside of their race. Many credit the rise in immigration and racial integration, which have increased the amount of contact that young adults have with people of different racial backgrounds, with the growing prevalence of interracial dating and marriage. Also, as a result of being raised during the civil rights era and the 1960s, many of today's parents have a much more liberal attitude toward interracial dating. However, although the Census Bureau statistics indicate a rapidly growing acceptance of couples who date across racial boundaries, there are a considerable number of people who do not accept interracial romance as a legitimate choice.

Cultural betrayal

Opponents of interracial dating contend that those who date or marry outside of their race are betraying their families and abandoning their cultural heritage. Many African Americans believe interracial marriage erodes the solidarity of the African American community. Author Lawrence Otis Graham feels that "interracial marriage undermines [African Americans'] ability to introduce our children to black role models who accept their racial identity with pride." Graham also fears that biracial children will turn their backs on their black heritage when they discover that it is easier to live as a white person.

Conservative whites oppose interracial marriage for a different reason. The rise in interracial births, combined with increased immigration, will make white people a minority by the middle of the twenty-first century. Some feel that this "browning of America" will lead to the eventual eradication of European-American culture. Syndicated columnist H. Millard believes that "we are seeing the death of the American and his replacement with a non-European type who now has enough mass in our society to pervert European-American ways." Millard also contends that if the current trend in interracial relationships and births continues, the white race will eventually become extinct. According to Millard, "white people . . . are going to have to struggle mightily to survive the Neo-Melting Pot and avoid being part of the one-size-fits-all human model. Call it what it is: Genocide and extinction of the white genotype."

A bridge across the racial divide

On the other hand, proponents of interracial relationships contend that interracial romance is a step toward eliminating racial hatred. According to Mitali Perkins, "Where exploitation and anger have separated the races in society, an interracial family called by God is a compelling example of the gospel of reconciliation." Yvette Walker believes that "racism . . . will have to be bred out. We can't make policies to change it. And certainly in an interracial relationship the children are raised in a climate of tolerance." She and others contend that the rising incidence of interracial children will eventually lead to a society where race will no longer matter because everyone will blend into one race, the human race. More importantly, assert many supporters of interracial relationships, color should not matter when it comes to love. They echo Martin Luther King Jr.'s famous sentiment that people should be judged not "by the color of their skin but by the content of their character."

The debate over interracial relationships is controversial because it touches on the sensitive areas of family, cultural heritage, religion, and racism. The diversity of views on this subject are reflected in *At Issue: Interracial Relationships*.

1

Interracial Marriage: An Overview

Clayton Majete

Clayton Majete is an instructor in the department of sociology and anthropology at Baruch College of the City University of New York.

Interracial relationships are still considered taboo as a result of misinformation. In the past, social scientists, and society in general, categorized people involved in interracial romances as disturbed, or they labeled these relationships as acts of rebellion against one's parents or attempts to move up the social ladder. However, scientific research on interracial marriage shows that this is not the case.

Interracial marriage in America may be the social institution that is least understood and most distorted by myth and bias. It should not surprise anyone that many of these biases are based on the racial divisions that permeate all aspects of our society. And although social science has studied practically every conceivable aspect of human relations, the interracial marriage remains remarkably understudied. Why do blacks and whites marry each other? How are their marriages different from or the same as same-race marriages? How do they overcome the overt racial prejudice in society to function in their relationships? These are questions I have been seeking answers to in my research with these couples.

To understand why interracial marriage is still so controversial requires a short history lesson. Although interracial marriage has existed in the United States since blacks first came to this country in the seventeenth century, it has always been considered a social taboo. Laws barring intermarriage between persons of color and whites existed in forty of the fifty states until 1967, when the U.S. Supreme Court ruled that these laws were unconstitutional. The number of black-white marriages rose just after blacks' emancipation and peaked around 1900. After a decline until 1940, the rates of intermarriage have been steadily increasing.

One reason for this increase is that the color line in the United States is changing. Desegregation throughout the 1970s increased the likelihood

From Clayton Majete, "What You May Not Know About Interracial Marriages." This article first appeared in the July 1997 issue of, and is reprinted with permission from, *The World & I*, a publication of The Washington Times Corporation; copyright ©1997.

that blacks and whites would interact more frequently on the job, in schools, and during leisure activities. All these factors would suggest an increase in interracial marriages, but interracial marriages accounted for only 0.33 percent of all marriages in 1980, according to the 1980 census. However, this rate reflects an increase from 0.09 percent in 1970. Based on the extrapolation of the 1980 census that was made in 1985, 1.2 percent of black women and 3.6 percent of black men marry out (black men have always married out more than black women). We know, however, that the actual rates of interracial marriage are greater than what is reflected in these census figures because many people find the census instructions difficult to use, and also many interracial couples refuse to report this on such forms.

Scientific research

Social scientists are as much to blame as anyone for the misinformation that exists about interracial marriage. Past research has focused on the supposed pathological aspects of the interracial relationship, assuming that anyone involved in such a relationship must be "disturbed" in some way. Social scientists have cited the need to rebel against parents or society, an affinity for the exotic or "forbidden fruit," blacks' desire to get even with the dominant culture, or whites' desire to atone for past racism as justifications for black-white marriage. Interracial marriage was justified for three general reasons: (1) the couple was pathological; (2) one partner was marrying to obtain a higher class or status than previously held, or (3) one or both partners were rebelling against their parents and/or society because of deep-seated resentment.

Although interracial marriage has existed in the United States since blacks first came to this country in the seventeenth century, it has always been considered a social taboo.

As part of my research on interracial couples, I asked them candid questions about their lives. The participants were solicited from advertisements in magazines and journals geared toward interracial couples. I also speak throughout the United States at clubs and organizations devoted to interracial relationships. Over two hundred couples volunteered to participate. For the most part they were well educated. Some 65 percent had undergraduate degrees, and 25 percent had obtained professional degrees and held positions as, for example, doctors, lawyers, nurses, and social workers. Ninety percent of couples were at the same level educationally. Although one might assume that these couples would aim for egalitarianism in their marriages, they displayed a traditional patriarchal marriage structure. Six out of ten women worked outside the home. Such being the case, the average household income placed these families solidly in the middle and upper-middle class.

These couples also came from middle-class families. Almost half the respondents met at work, college, or a social event. One couple met through a personal ad in a magazine that was geared toward interracial couples. Not surprisingly, about 20 percent of the couples in this study reported that they were friends or coworkers initially and their relationship developed into a romantic one. Work, school, and social events are racially integrated settings. As society becomes more desegregated in these areas of American life, we can expect that interracial encounters will increase, and with these an increase in the number of interracial marriages.

Over half the respondents in this study had not dated interracially prior to their current relationship. The black women, white men, and white women displayed a remarkable similarity in their history of no previous interracial dating prior to their current interracial relationship. The black men did have significantly more interracial dating experiences.

When it came to initiating an interracial relationship, among those in this study in 60 percent of the cases the white partner, male or female, took the lead. In comparison with the white, however, the black respondents had about twice as many family members who dated interracially. The family appears to have a significant influence for those involved in interracial relationships. Questions still to be answered are whether interracial dating by family members makes it more acceptable and whether that acceptance has to do with the racial attitudes and beliefs of the family or with some other, unknown dynamic.

Family reactions

In my research with interracial couples there are notable differences in the way black families and white families react to their children marrying someone of a different race. Almost three-quarters of the black families do not have a problem with their children marrying outside their race. Black families are usually more accepting of the interracial relationship and the white partner than white families are of the black partner. Often the interracial couple lives in a black or integrated community because of the disapproval they experience in all-white communities.

Three out of ten white families are not hostile about their children's relationship, but they do express concern. An example of a typical mixed reaction is that of a white mother who told her daughter to consider the effect such a relationship would have on her children. The mother was also concerned about what her friends would think, but the father had no problems. The mother did come around eventually, and the respondent said the wedding was a truly wonderful experience. One white man reported a similar situation. The family was initially hesitant, but, afraid of losing their son, they went along with it and became totally accepting of the relationship. These were typical of the mixed responses—an initial hesitation or rejection but an eventual change of mind after the parents realized that their children were serious about their relationship. Eighty percent of the parents expressed concern about possible children and the difficulty they would have in society. Several respondents said they felt that their parents did not want to meet their potential mates, because if they did they would come to like and accept them as part of the family.

The mixed response from one black woman's in-laws was typical. Her husband's family was polite most of the time and curt some of the time, but just not generally welcoming. Other respondents also reported this chilly reception from their white in-laws and recognized that some of their in-laws might simply be difficult to get along with no matter whom their child married. They mentioned that although an in-law may have seemed unaccepting of them, they were not sure if it was because of their race or the in-law's unpleasant personality.

Perhaps there is something we can learn from [interracial] families that can help us bridge the gap between the races in our society.

Other couples experienced outright hostility. The brother of one black woman said that if she brought her fiancé home to a family reunion, "he'd be sorry." She blamed her brothers for causing the breakup of her marriage to this man. The parents of one black woman disowned her. She said she felt as if she and her husband were "put on trial." A white man reported that he cannot bring his fiancé home, because his family is so angry at his choice. This family has not met his fiancé and apparently has no intention of doing so. Another white man said that he never told his parents about his black wife until he sent them a picture three months after the wedding. That was twenty-one years ago, and the parents still have not met their daughter-in-law. A white woman said her parents have never accepted her marriage, and she did not tell her parents that they had a grandchild for a year and a half.

One black woman reported that her husband's family took everything from him and disowned him, saying that they hated all blacks. Another black woman, whose father is currently in an interracial marriage and comes from a family that dates interracially, said that when she and her husband married, they did not tell his mother for fear of how she would react. For several respondents, the interracial marriage was a second marriage and their children or their spouse's children had difficulty with the marriage. One white man said the most difficult relationship was with his black wife's daughter, who has refused to accept their marriage.

Positive reactions

Conversely, other respondents reported positive reactions. One black woman said that her mother was "thrilled" and that, though her father had died before the wedding, he approved of the relationship. Another black woman said she did not get married until later in life, so her parents were "elated" when she married, period. One white woman felt that her family could not be more supportive, and they treat her husband as they do their other sons-in-law. A similar response came from a white woman whose sister was also married to a black man. Her mother was very supportive.

One black man's family was totally accepting of his marriage (this was not the first interracial marriage in the family), and since he knew his wife's family before he met her, they were also totally accepting of him. Both sets of in-laws socialized together.

One in three respondents mentioned that their families were either racist or nonprejudiced and felt that this had some bearing on how the family received their mate. A typical response was "that's the way my father is—a conservative southerner," and they felt little hope of changing their parents' beliefs. Others, who were raised to be more liberal and open-minded, were surprised that their parents were not more accepting of their mate. Another typical response was that parents who were initially hesitant eventually came to accept these relationships because they were concerned that if they cut off ties with their children, they would miss not only them but their grandchildren.

Although we might assume that interracial couples are rejected by their families, this is not always the case. Most families and in-laws are willing to at least accept their family member's interracial relationship, if not approve of it outright. Seventy-five percent of the couples had amicable if not very positive relationships with their parents. White women, however, received the most negative reactions from parents, and white men's and women's families had more difficulty accepting the interracial relationship. Of the relationships that were hostile, many appear to be irreconcilable. The respondents who were alienated from their parents appeared to want to have some relationship with them but had been rejected.

The stereotype of the rebellious child marrying someone of another race to hurt his or her parents appears to be just that—a stereotype. The respondents who were alienated from their family seemed neither rebellious nor pleased with the circumstances. Not one of them expressed satisfaction with their family situation. Some were angry, but most were resigned to their family's choices.

Overall, 75 percent of families seem to be open to interracial relationships, blacks more than whites. One concern for interracial families is that they would not have the support of an extended family, but the majority of these families were supported and accepted by the extended family. Among them, I did not get the sense of widespread isolation or emotional estrangement. Even those who had mixed reactions from their extended families still maintained some contact.

That these couples married for love may have something to do with their acceptance by family members. The positive aspects of these relationships need to be emphasized and further explored. How did the families who were initially reluctant come to terms with this issue? Why do some families have no difficulty accepting an interracial relationship? Perhaps there is something we can learn from these families that can help us bridge the gap between the races in our society. They have learned to love and accept their differences in ways that too few have.

Children of interracial couples

Over half the couples who had children mentioned that their parents were hesitant because of the potential effect on children. Polls show that most people who oppose interracial marriage do so because of the effect it will have on children. Yet the number of interracial births is steadily increasing, more than doubling from 21,400 (2.1 percent) in 1978 to 55,900 (3.9 percent) in 1992. These figures may be low, however, because the father's characteristics are not recorded for about 16 percent of all U.S. births and because some people do not report race on the census forms. The 1978 and

1992 rates reveal a significant increase above that in the 1970 census, which reported that 0.36 percent of births involved black and white parents. Nevertheless, the number of children in black-white households ranks third, below Asian-white and Hispanic-white households.

Currently, an estimated one million biracial children live in the United States, primarily in urban areas in the East, the Midwest, and the West Coast. In addition, the level of interracial marriage is expected to increase because of growth in the nonwhite population due to immigration, high birth rates, and lower mortality rates. Increased births of biracial children are also anticipated.

If interracial marriage is surrounded by bias, then biracial children have a double burden: bearing public reaction to their mixed parents as well as to their own mixed racial identity. Currently, the biracial child of black and white parents is considered black, a carryover from the days of slavery. The biracial identity of these children is ignored, and there is no such category listed by the U.S. Bureau of the Census. Biracial children have historically been perceived as having significant problems, such as ambiguous racial identity, rejection of one race, social marginality, and managing sexual impulses. There is no empirical evidence, however, to support these assumptions. No significant differences in adjustment have been found between children raised by same-race parents and those raised by mixed parents.

Children's racial identity

The question of racial identity remains a key issue in raising the biracial child. Most parents in the study used the term "biracial" to describe their child's race. One mother added that it was "a special race." The next most frequently used term was "mixed." Other parents described their children as "interracial," "mulatto," "white," and "black." One parent refused to describe her children, saying they were "whatever they want to be."

These parents are well aware of the conundrum of "categorizing" their biracial children. The white mother who reported her children's race as "biracial—a special race" noted that when she has to put down the race of her children she crosses out the categories and puts "biracial." However, she also acknowledged that her eight-year-old daughter sees herself as black. A black mother used the term "mixed" to describe her children's race, but then acknowledged that she considered them black.

The response of a black mother who described her seven-year-old daughter as "mulatto—maybe other" indicates how complicated this situation can be. Initially she said that she usually checks off "other" and puts down "brown" on a form. However, when the daughter is with her white father, he puts down "white." When she is with her black mother, the mother puts down "black." The daughter sees herself as brown.

A black mother with a two-year-old daughter expressed annoyance when asked about her child's race. When asked if she realized that any ascertainable sign of black says that you are black in our society, she replied, "I know that my child will have to be raised to realize that she is biracial and that other people will see her as black." She felt it was "evil" and "nonsense" to label her child.

A black mother with seventeen- and nineteen-year-old boys noted that the older son considers himself black, and the younger one mixed. The age of a child had a great deal to do with how parents spoke to their children about identity. One white mother of a four-year-old observed that her son was just becoming aware of race differences and that his father was black and his mother was white. He asked his parents what this made him. The mother has not told him anything specific, describing him in several different ways including "tan" and "biracial."

Because of their highly unusual status in society, these interracial families were very aware of the need to talk about race issues and how it affects their children.

A white mother with two young children refers to them as black. She sees this term as a political term—it bears no relevance to the way things really are. A black father classified his two daughters as white, and this is on their birth certificates.

Many parents mentioned that they have discussed racial issues with their children, stressing the importance of seeing people as individuals and not as blacks or whites. They wanted their children to know that there were differences, but that these differences did not matter when it came to what was inside a person.

All these parents have had to deal with the issue of identifying their children's race and apparently they have given a good deal of thought to it. Perhaps the dominant theme of this issue is that the parents do not have a label that adequately describes their children, not for the parents' sake but for society in general, which seems to need to label children. They recognized that their children would have to "check off" a certain category, and as far as they were concerned, there was no adequate category to describe their children's race.

Seven out of ten parents felt that their children had adjusted well to their biracial identity in school and with friends. The parents were well aware of racial prejudice and what their children would have to endure. One white father, who saw his daughter as biracial, acknowledged that she would have to learn to deal with racial conflict because society would see her as black. One black mother described a certain tension between her two daughters, now in their twenties, who looked different. One had blond hair and blue eyes, while the other had dark hair and dark eyes. The siblings would compare themselves and their experiences, and the darker daughter, according to the mother, had an identity crisis. The mother also pointed out that the daughters saw themselves as black and dated black men.

A black mother with older children in their thirties noted that her daughter has had difficulty because, although she does not look black, she wants to be black and wants to marry a black man. The daughter could pass for white and remarked that many of the white men she met did not know she had a black mother. When they discovered this fact, they stopped seeing her. The mother felt that her two children had it more difficult than most biracial children. Her son looked more like her, but the daughter looked more like her white father. This led to some role model confusion. However, the mother believed that her two children had a close relationship despite these differences.

Another black mother noted that some people use the term "biracial" to avoid using "black" to describe themselves. She pointed out that when some people list their race, black is always the last one to be mentioned. This same person acknowledged that an interracial relationship is probably more stressful than a same-race relationship, but she did not see this as a negative. She felt that her interracial relationship forced her to grow and to evaluate her values and society's values. This would make her a better person. She believed her children would benefit from their upbringing, also.

A black mother of one boy and three girls felt that her son had the most difficult time because of confusion about his identity. Her girls saw themselves as white. This was the mother who reported their race as "whatever they want it to be" but acknowledged that their legal status is black.

Although families were split on who would have a more difficult time adjusting to their biracial identity—males or females—families leaned toward the girls having more difficulty. They believed that girls would have more difficulty finding mates. Males were perceived to have more difficulty occupationally, that is, blacks did not have the same economic opportunities as whites. One white mother mentioned that society sees black men as threatening, which makes it more difficult for them.

Perhaps the major concern for parents in their children's adjustment to race and interracial parents was that they understood their children would be perceived as "different" and that they needed to be aware of the racism that they would eventually experience. Many of the parents with children in school or older have confronted racial incidents. Parents dealt with these issues by discussing with their children the reasons why some people act this way and how their children could handle it.

Developing a positive identity

Given the generally stable family relationships, the commitment to family life, and positive extended family relationships experienced by the parents of biracial children in my research, it appears that many of the concerns about biracial children are unfounded. These families reported that they were well aware of the need to develop a positive racial identity in their children. Indeed, the real hardship appears to be the labels imposed from outside the family and not from parents or extended family. The need to label these children was viewed as an imposition by society that had to be dealt with.

Because of their highly unusual status in society, these interracial families were very aware of the need to talk about race issues and how it affects their children. All the families I interviewed were open about race and the role it would play in their children's development. These parents were also candid about the difficulties their children would experience for no other reason than one of their parents was not white. Although some of the children were still too young to have to confront these issues, the parents of older children believed that their children had adjusted well because of how the parents handled these issues—by being open and honest. The families that had difficulties were frank about them.

Concerning religious affiliation, those interracial couples without children typically were not actively involved in church. Of those couples with children, however, 85 percent were affiliated with a religion and 65 percent have their children attend church or Sunday school on a regular basis. Although half reported no religious affiliation, most of those who did belonged to mainline religions such as Catholicism and Baptist. Thirty percent chose nonmainstream denominations such as Baha'i (which encourages interracial and interfaith marriages), Unitarian, and Pentecostal denominations. Seven out of ten of the couples reported different religious affiliations from their mate's. Thus, it appears that these respondents are religiously as well as racially diverse. Four couples in this study had severed ties with their congregations because they experienced prejudice and discrimination. It is not unusual for some couples to look for churches that welcome interracial couples. Ten percent of the respondents noted that they learned tolerance through their religious upbringing and wanted their children to learn it also.

Perhaps because [interracial couples] are forced to communicate on a different level about race, they have transcended many barriers that hold back others from interacting with people who are different from them racially.

Generally, these couples are a heterogeneous group. No characteristic stands out as homogeneous except for one—their political affiliation. Over 80 percent of the respondents reported belonging to the Democratic Party. About 8 percent were independents, but only 6 percent said that they were registered Republicans or that they voted Republican. However, close to 90 percent of the couples felt that political likemindedness was not important to their relationship. Over half did vote and were knowledgeable about political activities.

Overall, my impression of these couples is that they perceive themselves as rather ordinary and middle class, but they realize that society views them as an aberration. They have the same concerns about work, family, and getting ahead as other families. They never appeared to over-romanticize their situation, nor did they deny the harsh realities of the society they live in. I think that society's perceptions about who they are place greater stress on them than what is really occurring in the relationships. Society has imposed its point of view on these couples rather than allowed them to tell us how they are living their lives. This must place a great deal of stress on them, but most of them have handled it remarkably well. Perhaps because they are forced to communicate on a different level about race, they have transcended many barriers that hold back others from interacting with people who are different from them racially.

2

Interracial Relationships Can Help Overcome Racial Bias

Brian Marshall

Brian Marshall is a contributor to Interrace *magazine, a publication that focuses on issues pertaining to interracial couples and people.*

Becoming involved in an interracial relationship can help a person face the realities of racism. Interracial couples still elicit negative responses from the public, which is evidence of the racist feelings still present in American society. Interracial dating forces people to take an honest look at their feelings about race and confront their racial biases. Love can help people overcome these biases.

My parents knew that Tracy was black before I brought her over to the house.

I thought it only fair to tell them ahead of time, for their sakes as well as for Tracy's, so they wouldn't be caught standing there with their mouths hanging open, shocked and confused at the sight of their only son walking through the door with a black girl on his arm.

I had told them ahead of time with the hope that it would make the evening go more smoothly: free of trouble, free of embarrassment, and free of surprises. They seemed to take it well but I could picture them huddling together and discussing it amongst themselves, wondering how they were going to handle it, what they were going to do, and what they were going to say.

We were soon going to find out. I look over at Tracy sitting beside me, staring silently into the darkness at the fine mist illuminated by the headlights of the car. She's been quiet the whole twenty minutes we've been driving, saying little and sitting as still as if she were frozen. I know that her nerves must be wound pretty tight—I know mine sure are—and that her defenses are probably on full alert. I've told her again and again that it's going to be all right but I can't really be sure of that myself. I expel a

Reprinted from Brian Marshall, "The First to Cross," *Interrace*, Summer 1998, by permission of *Interrace*.

slow breath and put my eyes back out on the road, which lay black and wet before us.

It had been easier for me to meet her parents since she comes from a mixed background. But I was white, and my parents were white, and as far as I knew, my whole entire family was white and had had little to do with other ethnic groups. I was the first to cross the racial lines and it had been an uphill battle for me, fought mostly against myself and the stereotypical views and biases that I found were buried deep within my mind, carefully woven into my fabric of thinking where they lay dormant and unchallenged. Tracy had challenged those views and had left me scatterbrained, trying to fit together pieces that just didn't fit.

An uphill battle, indeed.

I had never imagined myself falling in love with a black woman, much less becoming romantically involved with one. But it had happened, and I had been forced to deal with it.

She had been in my Research and Design class, a second-year Sociology student like myself, and from the first time I saw her, I was instantly drawn, attracted to her quiet confidence and her sophisticated manner. She carried herself with style, a tall slender beauty with the most beautiful eyes I had ever seen: warm, sultry eyes, brown with flecks of green. I found myself staring at her, day dreaming, admiring her beauty, while the professor stood at the front of the classroom and rambled on about things I could care less about, his voice sounding like it was a million miles away. But she was black. And I was white. And nowhere in my world did I see the two coming together.

We were paired together for a project and I was amazed at how quickly we hit it off, spending most of our research time talking and laughing. I felt comfortable around her. We liked the same movies; the same books; the same foods. I couldn't believe how much we had in common. I got her phone number and I called her, pretending to be concerned about some aspect of our project, but really just wanting to talk to her and hear her voice.

I had never imagined myself falling in love with a black woman. . . . But it had happened.

Then one day I asked her out to dinner without thinking about what I was saying, not realizing until after she had accepted and the date was made what I had done. For a split second I thought about canceling but I just couldn't bring myself to do it. I mean, as weird as it seemed to me, I really wanted to see this girl.

That first date I was nervous as hell, jittery, self conscious, tense—you name it. I was aware of people watching us as we made our way to the table. I'd picked an upscale restaurant and most of the diners were middle-aged businessmen and their wives. At first, their looks didn't bother me too much, but I became rattled when I noticed that some of their looks were ones of disapproval. It wasn't blatant, but I could sense it like a bad smell. A hush came over certain tables as we passed and then the inevitable buzz of quiet conversation.

I had the feeling that Tracy could sense my discomfort but I did my best to hide it, acting cool and relaxed when in reality my insides were clenching and unclenching like a tight fist. I could barely eat. But somehow, with the magic of her eyes and the soft, smooth warmness of her voice, I managed to forget about the other patrons and what they were thinking and we made a second date. And a third. And a fourth.

And each time we went out, I found my levels of self-consciousness getting less and less. It didn't go away completely; there were times I would catch a reflection of ourselves in a mirror somewhere and I would feel myself tense, seeing us as the world saw us: black and white.

And now here we were: four months into a steady relationship, planning a future together, and very much in love.

We're getting closer to the house now and the only sound is the squeak of the wipers as they swish from side to side. It's started to rain since we left Tracy's and it only serves to make the night more ominous, more threatening. I'm wondering what my parents are going to say tonight. My mind keeps re-playing the same ugly scenarios over and over, each one ending with a common conclusion: disaster. I try to think positive.

There were times I would catch a reflection of ourselves in a mirror . . . and I would feel myself tense, seeing us as the world saw us: black and white.

My parents aren't racist by any means, but they are ignorant, and I wonder if the two aren't really the same thing. I hope that their concern for me, however misguided it may be, doesn't gestate into subtle hostility for Tracy. I hope they understand that this relationship is serious and not just some experiment in curiosity, not some phase that I'll grow out of after I find some nice white girl to "really" settle down with. I hope for a lot of things.

"You know," I say, breaking the silence. "It doesn't matter what they think. Whether they approve or not, it doesn't matter."

She looks at me with her soft brown eyes. "I know," she says quietly, almost in a whisper. Her hand comes out of the darkness and rests on my knee. Its presence there suddenly soothes me and I feel better, more secure, the way I always do when she touches me.

I remember how tough I used to act when we used to walk through shopping malls, at a stage when I was still trying to get used to being with her, looking straight into everybody's eyes and just silently daring them to say something, anything. I wanted a challenge. I wanted a fight. I wanted to prove that I was serious. But all I was doing was masking my fear, my own insecurity with what I was doing.

Deep down I cared what people thought. And I had fear. A constant gnawing fear that sometimes left me cold, wanting to back out, wanting to run, wanting to go where I was safe, where I was accepted. It ate me from the inside and as a man I felt ashamed for being afraid. Afraid of the back lash. Afraid of what people were thinking. Afraid that I wouldn't have the guts or the courage to stick it out. Afraid because my world was changing and opening up.

And that's where the solution to my problem lay. Before I met Tracy I was going through life with blinders on, oblivious to the struggles going on around me, not caring about an issue unless it affected my life directly. And that's where I had been wrong. So very, very wrong.

I learned that racism was a living breathing thing and not just some word in a newspaper. It wasn't just some excuse that people used to explain their failures. It had claws and it could bite. It was real. And for the first time in my life I was seeing the struggles that I had been blind to all along, and now, as my eyes were opened, I found myself involved in the struggle, with Tracy standing firmly by my side.

It was as if I had been in the dark my whole life, trapped in a bubble, and now suddenly the bubble burst and I was free, eyes open to a world I'd never known before.

There were never any doubts after that. I had been sitting too comfortably in a world of ignorance and indifference for far too long. If it hadn't been for Tracy, I would still be walking around in that same mental fog, breathing that same stale air, letting my thoughts and my feelings be shaped by others. She changed me for the better. Of that I am sure.

We pull into the driveway of my parents' house and I take a deep breath.

"We're here," I say. "Are you ready?"

She looks at me and smiles. Nervously. "As ready as I'm ever going to be."

As we walk up the stairs to the front door I am aware that we will be walking the edges of acceptance wherever we go, and that we probably will be for the rest of our lives. But it doesn't matter. I know that walls are not solid, impenetrable things—they can tumble down. And people can change. And I know that we have come closer to knowing the true nature of God than any of the bible-quoting zealots who condemn us.

It's all about love.

It's that pure and it's that simple.

And I don't walk afraid anymore.

I hold her hand and I walk proud.

3
Interracial Marriages Alone Will Not Eliminate Racism

Eric Liu

Eric Liu is a regular contributor to USA Today *and MSNBC. He has served as a speechwriter for President Clinton and he is the author of* The Accidental Asian: Notes of a Native Speaker.

Social critics as far back as Alexis de Tocqueville have proclaimed that intermarriage is the only true path to healing racial strife in America. However, while interracial marriage is a powerful symbol of love transcending racial barriers, it does not have a substantial effect on racism. Despite increasing numbers of interracial families, racial stereotypes, such as the belief that lighter skin color is more desirable, are still prevalent.

Sometimes, as my wife and I walk down the street, we'll notice a couple coming the other way. We won't do anything to indicate that we've seen them. We won't make eye contact. But immediately after they pass, Carroll and I will give each other a nudge.

"BRC," we'll whisper. As in "biracial couple."

Now, this may sound a little odd. Or unduly color-conscious. Or maybe even prejudiced. But you see, it isn't with disapproval that we notice BRCs. After all, we are one. Carroll is Scotch-Irish and Jewish; I am Chinese. And we are conscious of other mixed couples. We practically tally them up because there's something undeniably satisfying about encountering fellow trespassers of the color line.

For one thing, there's a sense of solidarity, the feeling that this other couple might know, on some level, how we relate to the world. There's also, I have to say, a sense of confidence, perhaps even smugness, a feeling that we are the wave of the future, ahead of the demographic curve.

There was a time, of course, when racial intermarriage was strictly prohibited, whether by law or by custom. And to be sure, most marriages today are still unmixed. But Americans are intermarrying more today

Reprinted from Eric Liu, "Mingling Bloodlines Isn't Enough to Bridge the Race Gap," *USA Today*, June 11, 1998, by permission of the author.

than ever before. The number of mixed-race unions has increased from 150,000 in 1960 to over 1.5 million in 1998; the number of multiracial kids has boomed to more than 2 million.

And so it's not surprising that one of the central points of Warren Beatty's farcical film *Bulworth* is that mixing up our genes (Sen. Bulworth puts it more colorfully) is the way to move the country beyond color. As Beatty said in an interview, there's a simple solution to the race problem: "It's called love."

This "love" line is an old riff. Throughout our history, people from Alexis De Tocqueville to Frederick Douglass to Norman Podhoretz have proclaimed that miscegenation is the only true path to interracial healing.

It's certainly a nice thought. As one who has jumped into the integrated gene pool, I'd like to think I'm doing my part to advance good race relations. But it's misguided, in the end, to say that the difference I make is the difference that matters.

We can start by asking a simple question: What is the problem that intermarriage is supposed to solve? If the problem is strife between races, well sure, BRCs are powerful symbols of life beyond pure hostility. But generally, BRCs aren't trying to save the world; they just happened to fall in love. And their mere existence doesn't do much to alter the social circumstances—from residential segregation to media stereotypes to campaign rhetoric—that can generate racial hostility.

If the problem is something else—say, that people of color are vulnerable to discrimination—it's not clear that BRCs solve the problem at all. It's true, of course, that mixed marriages produce mixed kids and that mixed children defy old racial categories. It's not necessarily true, though, that the collapse of racial categories means the collapse of racialism.

Let's not forget that when it comes to bridging the gap of race, love isn't all we need.

Consider how "blacks," who are as genetically mixed a group as can be found in America, were converted by a "one-drop rule" into a single group. Think about how those Asian-Americans who are assimilating and intermarrying are said now to be "becoming white."

And note that while intermarriage is up across the board, mixed marriages involving blacks are still the least common.

Perhaps our color line is giving way to a color continuum. But life along that continuum is still likely to follow a simple rule: The lighter you are, the better. When Carroll and I have kids, will they be considered white? Will they be called Asian? Will they be more stigmatized than "pure" whites and Asians? Will they be less stigmatized than other mixed children with darker skin?

The answers lie not in what is to be seen but in how people choose to see. Intermarriage isn't the panacea we'd like it to be, but it does make one thing clear: Race is a man-made myth, not a God-given truth, and it's something we impose upon each other often in spite of our actual color.

That's why it falls to that other timeless pursuit—politics, rather than procreation—to address the fact that in countless unwanted ways, race still matters. It's in the realm of public life, not the realm of personal romance, that we can do most to equalize the life chances of kids of every hue.

So by all means, let's mingle our blood lines with abandon. Let's hurry forth the day when counting BRCs is a tired game. But let's not forget that when it comes to bridging the gap of race, love isn't all we need.

4

Interracial Marriage Is a Step Toward a More Integrated Culture

Scott London

Scott London is the host of Insight & Outlook, *a syndicated cultural affairs radio program.*

Interracial relationships are a step toward a more integrated and egalitarian society. The future of America belongs to the person who is the product of many different cultures. Through interracial marriage, different cultures will develop their unique identities and come together in harmony.

Some years ago *Time* magazine published a special issue on multiculturalism in America. The cover featured a beguiling mestizo woman over the caption "The New Face of America." The cover girl was at once familiar and exotic. With her placid smile and somewhat ambiguous features, she looked like someone you might encounter in tomorrow's Los Angeles or Toronto—a curious melange of Asian, Middle Eastern, African, and Anglo-Saxon traits.

As it happened, *Time's* model was not a real person but a cybernetic crossbreed. The image was created on a computer by "morphing" men and women from various racial and ethnic backgrounds. As *Time's* editors explained, this was a preview of the sort of offspring likely to emerge in tomorrow's multicultural society.

The magazine cover captured an essential truth about America at century's end. We live in an increasingly diverse and increasingly mongrel society, a nation of blurred boundaries and bizarre extremes. Never before in history has a society been as diverse as the U.S. is today. And never before have so many different traditions, beliefs and values been integrated into a single culture.

For all the platitudes about melting pots, mosaics, and rainbow coalitions, many regard the "browning" of America as a profoundly disturbing

Reprinted from Scott London, "The Face of Tomorrow: Reflections on Diversity in America," *HopeDance*, September/October 1998, by permission of the author.

trend. Miscegenation is still regarded as culturally taboo on Main Street. As recently as 20 years ago, some states still had laws in place forbidding interracial marriage.

Many people complain that miscegenation waters down their culture. Some Jews, for example, blame the disintegration of Judaism on the growing rate of interfaith marriages in America. Similarly, a number of Indian tribes are concerned that thinning bloodlines will lead to the "statistical extermination" of their people. A century ago, half of all Indians in the U.S. were considered fullbloods. Today the number is down to about 20 percent. On Indian reservations, there is now a suicide problem among young half-breeds who don't feel sufficiently "pure."

As writer Richard Rodriguez has pointed out, we have never had an especially rich vocabulary for miscegenation. While other cultures speak of themselves as mestizos, mulattoes, and creoles, we persist in referring to ourselves using clumsy designations like Asian-American, African-American, Native American, and even Anglo-American. Curiously, the 1990 census form had boxes for "white," "black" and "other," but not for "multiracial." Bureaucrats in Washington are now preparing a form for the 2000 census. How about a box for "all of the above"? Or, better yet, how about no boxes for race?

Some say that America is actually less diverse than it was a century ago. There is some truth to this. A hundred years ago one could stroll along the wharves of New York City and hear a dozen languages and encounter immigrants from every corner of the old world. But this argument hides an essential fact: the main reason America is less diverse today than it was at the turn of the century is because of all the criss-crossing that has occurred in the intervening generations. We are no longer a nation of Scandinavian farmers, Chinese laborers, and Polish merchants, we are a nation of crossbreeds. In the last two decades alone, the number of intermarriages in the U.S. has jumped from 300,000 to over a million. The incidence of births of mixed-race babies has multiplied 26 times as fast as that of any other group.

The mingling and the mixing of race is a sign that we are evolving toward a higher, more integrated state as a culture.

These facts are sobering in light of all the divisive talk of cultural separatism and resurgent ethnic pride in America. After the Los Angeles riots, it was common to hear pundits lament the deepening "racial divide" in the United States. Some wrote portentously about how the nation was splitting into two parts, one white and one black. There is a certain arrogance in these assertions for they always assume that whites and blacks are at the center of the racial equation. It's as though whites and blacks can imagine America only in terms of each other. The truth is that many of the racial tensions in America have nothing to do with blacks or whites. In some parts of Los Angeles, for example, the worst gang violence involves Mexicans, Hmongs, and Koreans. In San Francisco high schools, the fight is between Filipinos and Samoans.

As I see it, the mingling and the mixing of race is a sign that we are evolving toward a higher, more integrated state as a culture. One indication of this is the fact that, as the French theologian Teilhard de Chardin put it, "union differentiates." The smaller the differences are between people, the more they insist on them. Anthropologists have long observed that as people and cultures evolve, they become more and more distinctive. They don't shed the qualities that make them unique, they refine and develop them. Diversity appears to be a function of social evolution.

Of course, diversity doesn't mean a thing if it doesn't challenge us to be more open-minded and inclusive. All too often, what passes for diversity are merely brown, black, and white versions of the same political ideology. There will always be those who overemphasize our diversity and fail to appreciate our essential unity, just as there will always be those who overemphasize our unity and fail to recognize the virtues of diversity. It's a delicate balance.

Our founding fathers captured this tension in our national motto, *E Pluribus Unum*—from the many, one. It's the great paradox of America: what we have in common is diversity. When the founders laid out America's first principles two hundred years ago, they took inspiration from the Iroquois Indian Confederacy. The Indian tribes modelled this principle of unity in diversity by retaining their individuality while at the same time belonging to a common network in the name of progress and mutual protection.

As we look to the 21st century, we are faced with the very same challenge: how do we recognize our fundamental unity without brushing aside the important differences that make us separate and distinct?

One way to do this was suggested to me by philosopher Barbara Marx Hubbard. She feels that an enlightened society ought to ask each group or culture to contribute what it considers its unique gift. "Make uniqueness a blessing," she said. If we were to do this, in very short order people would cease to speak of themselves as blacks or whites or straights or gays or Buddhists or Christians. Instead, they would begin to speak of themselves as individuals—as ethnicities and denominations of one. People would no longer want to be lumped together in groups, except to the extent that they share a common vision.

It's not as far-fetched as it sounds. We find this same principle at work in sports teams, business groups and community organizations. As any good leader knows, group success hinges on making the best use of people's unique talents and abilities.

In 1782 Crèvecoeur famously observed that in America "individuals of all nations are melted into a new race." The question then as now is, will the obliteration of certain distinctions mean the obliteration of identity itself?

I don't think so. I look upon the hybridization of America as a source of great promise. The future belongs to the mestizo, the person who straddles many different worlds and can help explain them to each other.

5

Interracial Marriage Is Genocide

Kevin Alfred Strom

Kevin Alfred Strom is the host of the radio program American Dissi-dent Voices. *This program is funded by the National Alliance, an organization that promotes the advancement and protection of the white race.*

The birthrate of mixed-race children is rising steadily, while the birthrate for white children continues to drop. If the prevalence of interracial marriage and mating continues, the white race will eventually become extinct. Men and women of European lineage who enter into unions with members of other races are polluting the European gene pool. By marrying outside of the white race, they are contributing to the genocide of their people and the extinction of their culture.

L et me read you a short article published in *Harper's Magazine*, which is controlled by the super-rich MacArthur family, whose John D. and Katherine T. MacArthur Foundation is almost omnipresent as the opening and closing sponsor of so-called "public television" programs. The article, written by David A. Bush, is headlined "Ozone Anxiety: It's a White Thing":

> A lot has been said recently about the thinning of the ozone layer. Interestingly, it turns out that the whole issue is really of concern only to fair-skinned Caucasians in the Northern Hemisphere, who are threatened with skin cancer and other problems associated with increased ultraviolet radiation. The peoples of the middle latitudes have always been exposed to higher ambient levels of ultraviolet radiation, but their naturally darker skin has acted as protection. It is entirely possible that "lard-white" skin just will not make it in this new world reality! Perhaps the era of the "classic" Caucasian is drawing to a close, and for completely natural reasons. Fair skin might eventually be considered an affliction

Reprinted from Kevin Alfred Strom, "Racemixing: Worse Than Murder," *Free Speech*, January 1996, by permission of National Vanguard Books.

and impose on those who possess it severe limitations on their enjoyment of the world.

The far-thinking Caucasian cannot help but realize that the best gift delicate-skinned individuals can give their progeny is a better chance of survival in the coming ultraviolet environment. Fair-skinned individuals should give careful consideration to the selection of a mate who will contribute a darker complexion to the genetic makeup of their offspring.

I am not suggesting that the government should mandate changes, but it could do a great deal to encourage interracial coupling. First of all, the government could provide some financial incentive to encourage interracial families. Special tax deductions would mitigate some of the problems that these families encounter.

On another level, the government could organize summer camps, or even working camps, where majority children would encounter minority children in a relaxed atmosphere, away from social constraints.

Let me add that when the author says "away from social constraints," what he really means is away from parents and away from peers of the opposite sex and the same race, whose instinctive abhorrence for interracial coupling might "inhibit" the results desired by the author and presumably by *Harper's Magazine* and the MacArthur family. Now back to the *Harper's* article:

Majority girls would participate in camps where they would encounter only minority boys, and vice versa. In such an environment, children would not be subjected to prejudicial pressures or obsolete taboos. Even if relationships did not develop at these camps, the participants would gain a greater appreciation of people who are different from themselves. When they returned home, they might be more disposed to the idea of a different-race partner.

In addition, the public should be educated about the positive aspects of a darker complexion. When mainstream television programming promotes the existence of couples from different races and backgrounds, then cultural and racist barriers will fall and society will move forward. A major benefit will be the fact that the population's general resistance to ultraviolet radiation will be enhanced.

The thinning of the ozone layer is just one more reason for Caucasian parents to bestow the gift of a darker complexion on their offspring. If we continue to lose the ozone, there may not be any options at all for fair-skinned individuals, as they will simply cease to exist. But if Caucasians do the right thing, how comforting it will be for them to look at their children and know they have done their best to ensure them a safe and comfortable future.

The genocide of the white race

Harper's Magazine published that article in December 1993. It had originally been printed by a glossy magazine called *Interrace*, the primary purpose of which is to promote interracial sex and marriage. We do not know the source of the funding for *Interrace* magazine, but we do know that its reported owner is a person named "Candace Mills" and the list of its officers consists of only one name repeated for each position, and that name is "Gabe Grosz."

Now David A. Bush may know, and the MacArthur family surely knows that what they are calling for is genocide of the White race. And all of them surely know that their moronic argument about reducing the rate of skin cancer by a minuscule amount is not the real motivation for their call to exterminate our people.

Here we have a major pillar of the liberal establishment calling far more openly for a genocide far more sweeping than that they accuse Adolf Hitler of calling for. And yet we hear of no protests against *Harper's* or its owners, no Million Man Marches of White men and women concerned for the survival and welfare of their kind, no charges of "hate crimes" against the perpetrators of this outrage. No. We hear nothing except a few worried clucks from conservatives that, well, "they probably don't really mean it that way," and approving snickers from Jews and White liberals about how amusing it all is and how wonderful and advanced their thinking is on such matters. Well, I don't think it's funny, and I do think they mean it, and we ought to take this advocacy of genocide through racial mixture very seriously indeed. We must take it seriously because it is happening right now.

Worse than murder

Under the title "Interracial Baby Boom," the following data from the Population Reference Bureau was published in *The Futurist:*

> Between 1968 and 1989, children born to parents of different races increased from 1% of total births to 3.4%. U.S. Census Bureau data show that, mirroring changes in laws and attitudes from 1970 to 1991, the number of mixed-race married couples increased from 310,000 to 994,000. PRB researchers observe that this trend is taking place among all racial and ethnic groups, but the patterns for each group are distinctly different.

The article goes on to say that although mixed marriages still represented less than four per cent of the total in 1989, the trend is definitely upward, tripling in less than twenty years. And that trend is probably accelerating. Carry that four per cent forward a few decades—three times four is 12, three times 12 is 36, and three times 36. . . . Couple this ominous trend with the fact that the White birth rate is now below the replacement level, and you see that use of the term genocide is not hyperbole. Also carefully consider this, according to the Population Reference Bureau report: "Most mixed births involve one white parent, but by no means all."

Notice the use of the qualifying words, "but by no means all." Why add them? Out of 994,000 mixed race couples, would anyone expect that every single one of them that had a child would have one White parent? Of course "by no means all." But the extremely significant thing to notice is the report's admission that most mixed births involve one White parent. What does this mean? It means that the majority of racial mixing involves the destruction of the White race—Whites mating with Asians, Whites mating with Blacks, Whites mating with Arabs or Jews, Whites mating with *mestizos*, Whites mating with the racially unclassifiable. You have seen it in your shopping centers. You have seen it in the street. You are a witness to genocide. You are seeing it before your very eyes every day. What are you doing about it? If you do not at least speak out against it, you are allowing yourself to be complicit in this horrible crime.

The majority of racial mixing involves the destruction of the White race.

The crime is racemixing. It is a worse crime than murder—far worse.

For when you commit murder you kill one man, you end one life, you tragically injure one family and circle of friends. When you commit murder, if your victim has had no children you do cut off the potential existence of one small branch of the race's future.

But when you commit the crime of racial mixing you are participating in genocide. The probable effect and possible motive for your act is to bring into the world hybrid young, who will not be clearly of one race or the other and which will, by their very existence, increase the probability of future racial mixing and dilute both the gene pool and the sense of identity of the next generation of White children. And don't underestimate the importance of that instinctive sense of identity among our young Whites. Except for efforts like this radio program, which are growing but are still far too small, that sense of identity is about the only thing standing between us and total extinction of the European race. Our young people may be confused, but their innate sense of decency and racial identity has held amazingly firm so far. Even though the Jewish media have been strenuously promoting interracial sex for decades, and even though the so-called "White establishment" has provided no leadership and nothing but treason to our race for the last 30 years and more, about 90 per cent of them are still marrying within their race. This contrasts starkly with the results of a recent *Washington Post* poll on the subject. According to the poll results, only 47 per cent of White men would not be willing to marry a Black woman; and only 60 per cent of White women would be unwilling to marry a Black man. Quite clearly there is a gap between what White people say and what they actually do. Why? Even among those intimidated into responding to the question in a Politically Correct manner—

even among those who have at some level convinced themselves that they would mate with any arguably human subspecies—the natural instinct to cleave to your own kind is still a powerful determinant of action. Thank God that it is! And to Hell with those who are working in the media and in the schools and in the churches to destroy that healthy natural tendency in our children. They are worse than murderers.

The propaganda of genocide

And yes, you heard me right, some of these murderers of our future generations have weaseled their way into positions of influence in the churches. That many of these have hidden Communist sympathies or are actually in the pay of our enemies has been documented by many others, and I do not have the time to recapitulate those data today. But their words speak for themselves. Let me give you a few quotations from the March 1994 issue of *Christianity Today*, a mainstream Protestant publication.

> . . . Is it possible God actually calls some Blacks to fall in love with Whites, and vice-versa? If that is true, then we should celebrate.

> Yes, celebrate! Let's rejoice over the beautiful children born to interracial marriages and do everything possible to make them fully accepted. Let's recognize the contributions intermarriage can make toward breaking down prejudice. And though we may not necessarily promote interracial marriages, let's take the lead in defending, protecting, and supporting them in our churches.

> . . . The entertainment industry has attempted to keep pace with the increasing number of intermarrying Americans. Television shows such as *General Hospital* and *L.A. Law* and major Hollywood releases like *Jungle Fever*, *Mississippi Masala*, *The Joy Luck Club*, and *The Bodyguard* have all highlighted interracial romances.

> This is one area where the media may be morally ahead of the church.

> . . . American churches can become havens of safety and support for interracial couples. . . . More creative heterogeneous churches may emerge, becoming places that feel like home to interracial families. . . . We should rejoice over the barrier-shattering potential each Christian interracial marriage brings to our churches.

That is what it says in the March 1994 issue of *Christianity Today*, the chairman of the board and founder of which is the Reverend Billy Graham. No comment should be necessary. I invite you to obtain a copy from your local library if you think I am misrepresenting their position.

Every White man who commits the crime of marrying a non-White will not be fathering any White children. Every White woman who pollutes her body and her spirit by marrying a non-White will not be giving birth to any White children. And by their actions they will be committing the crime of misleading White boys and girls to follow their example. And all those who do not speak out against their racial treason will be complicit in the crime. When your four-year-old sees a Black or an Asian or a *mestizo* with a White mate, and you do not condemn this, that child will believe that what he has seen is normal and that his mommy and daddy approve of it.

Nature—or Nature's God if you prefer to express it that way—created our race through hundreds of thousands of years of incredible hardship and rigorous selection. We have survived the Ice Ages. We have fought against invaders for thousands of generations, from the Moors to the Huns, again and again and again, back beyond the impenetrable mists of history of our race. Our ancestors gave their all so that we might survive, so that we might live. And we *do* live. We *did* survive. Thanks to them. Our race extends back continuously to the mysterious beginning of life itself. It can extend into the infinite future. And its continued existence would undoubtedly be assured by our superior intelligence and unmatched technology, if it were not for those who practice and promote the genocide of our people through racial mixing. By their actions they are killing us. They kill not an individual. They kill the infinite generations of our future. Their crime—the crime of racial mixture—is far, far worse than mere murder.

When you commit the crime of racial mixing you are participating in genocide.

As long as I live, I will be shouting this truth from the housetops and doing everything I can to encourage more and more of my people to see this truth. And I will applaud the growing numbers of members of other races who understand that racial mixing means death for their race and culture as well. This truth is the one factor that the promoters of the one world government called the New World Order fear. They do not fear the constitutionalist and the legalist "patriots" who avoid the issue of race in order to gain for themselves a measure of "respectability." They do not fear the sellers of gold coins on radio station WWCR. They don't care how many sacks of gold and silver coins you have salted away. They don't care if the front men for their secret government call themselves conservatives or liberals. They don't care if there is prayer in the schools or not. The one thing they fear more than anything else is racial consciousness, because they know their history, because they know that national and racial loyalty threaten their plan to establish the ultimate multicultural construct, a world government. For this twisted dream of world dominion, they are attempting genocide against our people.

6

The Bible Prohibits Interracial Marriage

Paul Hall

Paul Hall is editor and publisher of the Jubilee, *a newspaper that focuses on topics pertinent to American Christian patriots.*

When God created the different races of the world, He intended for them to remain separate. Those who marry across racial lines are breaking the laws that God made explicit in the Bible. The mixing of the races is responsible for the corruption of America and will eventually lead to the extinction of the White race.

Having had the opportunity to be out and about a bit this summer, I noticed more young people with members of the opposite sex who were not racial peers.

Before I continue—all those who classify the word *race* as an emotional buzzword and who are already conjuring up pre-programmed, inaccurate synonyms like "hate," "intolerance," "bigot," etc., I'd ask you to be tolerant for a few minutes before mentally dismissing my commentary. And, do keep in mind that [President Bill Clinton] Klinton himself has asked for this discussion. . . .

So as I was saying, I've noticed more interracial couples meandering about this summer. Television (if you watch it) has been "showing" America how to "do it" for years and it would seem people are starting to catch on.

When you hear the word "genocide" you typically think of the mass murder of people such as the 20 million Russians killed by Edomite dictators in Russia. Or today, Christians might think of the 4000 babies being aborted every day.

Interracial marriage is mass murder

What I want to bring to your attention is the mass murder of a nation of people through the process of giving birth.

Most Christians can see the effects of abortion (aborticide) and are

Reprinted from Paul Hall, "Interracial Genocide," *Jubilee*, July/August 1997, by permission of the author.

saddened by it. We are appalled by the deaths of young (and old) via the Klintonesta drug cartel. We are sickened by the suicide rate of our children through the influences of rock music idols. Christians can *see* these things happening daily and daily we talk about it at gatherings, on radio and in our periodicals.

But not much is said about the huge problem of interracial genocide, the destruction of God's Children (and ALL RACES of people) through integration. The destruction of culture, heritage, and race is not given much thought! In fact, racial heritage is simply not an issue for the majority of Christians. The Bible's direct instruction and law on the subject has been ignored or dismissed as "outdated."

The epidemic of interracial children is the systematic and planned extermination of an entire racial group—the main target is the "evil" white man.

The Bible's direct instruction and law on [interracial marriage] has been ignored or dismissed as "outdated."

Just as sorrowful is the fact that such unholy unions destroy the purity of the other race involved. God made man and said it was good. He made different races of people and gave them their own attributes, cultures, languages, lands and even allowed them to worship freely.

It has largely remained this way for centuries. Even today you'll notice Japanese in Japan do not intermarry. Very infrequently will you notice a Japanese person married to another race. Why? (Except Japanese-American kids who have been separated from their native culture and are "MTVed" and/or public school educated.)

Many Christian churches rail against the United Nations while unwittingly encouraging their flock to fall into its trap. You see, the UN building itself houses a statue of a genderless person in its rotunda that exemplifies its idea of future humanity: It has no specific racial characteristics, it's black in color representing a racially mixed person; it's their concept of the global human with a global religion (humanism) and no nationalist ideals.

Just ask yourself, whose idea was this multiracial marriage thing anyway? Ask your grandparents what society thought of interracial marriages when they were young. It was illegal in most states.

God's law has not changed

Unlike a few short years ago, integration is no longer discouraged since most pastors believe God's Law prohibiting the sin has been done away with or that God somehow changed his mind after the Cross. Not true! "For I *am* the LORD, I change not; therefore ye sons of Jacob are not consumed."—Malachi 3:6. See also Matthew 5:17: "Think not that I am come to destroy the Law, or the prophets: I am not come to destroy, but to fulfill."

While the Bible teaches that non-Israelites can (and will ultimately) worship God and receive the blessings of obedience this is not a valid reason to destroy what God created and called good by intermarrying with other races. Do cats mate with lions? Why not?

The enemies of Yahweh know that by dissolving the white (Israelite) culture and race they can destroy Israel's Spiritual/Covenantal relationship with God. Modern Christian Israelites are the Covenant people—the people Yahweh has chosen to administer his Law and establish His Kingdom (1 Peter 2:9).

Israel was to be a blessing to other nations, but as she disappears so do the blessings (Genesis 28:14; Romans 8:21–22).

You may not like these facts as they probably go against your public school and Judeo-church upbringing, but the substantiating evidence is overwhelming.

The systematic and planned extermination of an entire national, racial, political, or ethnic group is what has been before us as a people. More whites are dying everyday through interracial offspring than all the wars, abortions, accidents, and natural deaths put together. It's called interracial genocide. And, it doesn't stop with a single generation, it eliminates the opportunity for offspring to fulfill the role as God's covenant people for many generations (Genesis 28:4). God's People Israel are *not* simply spiritual believers. (The phrase "My people Israel" appears 28 times in the Bible and refers to the literal descendants of Jacob.)

Recent statistics show the white male is literally disappearing from America. By 2010 whites are projected to be the minority. By 2000 the white male will comprise about 40% of the work force. (Check out Deuteronomy 28:43, 44, 48 and Lamentations 5:12.) In many cities whites are already the minority.

Each half-white child born amounts to nothing less than the systematic elimination of yet another of God's Children.

Whites are not vanishing at this alarming rate due only to abortion and natural death; interracial genocide is a major contributor (zero population growth rate). That is *why* we have epidemic levels of immigration from third world countries and why we had bussing, affirmative action, and all the rest of the social engineering—to integrate whitey out of existence or at least to a controllable level.

If you were fighting a war wouldn't you want to destroy your enemy's troops? Now you're starting to see the picture.

I stress, although he is the target, it's not just the white man who is being bred out of existence. Other races constantly demand "racial/ cultural recognition" but ironically their race and cultures are being destroyed just as quickly as the whites.

Do not be made to feel guilty for having pride in your race (no matter what it is). It is *not* "cool" to marry a "person of color." Nor is it cool for non-whites to marry a white person.

And let this sink in: Yahweh does not care how much you "love" someone or how much you have in common, no more than He would care how much I may dislike someone—if I killed that person it would be murder. Likewise, marrying outside of your race is just as wrong regardless of your feelings.

Each half-white child born amounts to nothing less than the systematic elimination of yet another of God's Children. Integration is tantamount to aborting the holy seed of God.

Don't be upset with me and call me a bunch of pre-programmed names. It's not my "interpretation," "own religious beliefs," or "twisted account of scripture to fit my racist beliefs," it's God's law.

Biblical evidence

In case you missed the passages dealing with the sin of interracial marriages here are a few you should read. Ezra chapters 9 and 10 explains how God's People Israel were to deal with their non-Israelite wives and mixed children:

- "The people of Israel, and the priests, and the Levites, have not separated themselves from the people of the lands, *doing* according to their *abominations.*
- "For they have taken of their daughters for themselves, and for their sons: so that *the holy seed* have mingled themselves with the people of *those* lands: yea, the hand of the princes and rulers hath been chief in this *trespass.*
- "And now, O our God, what shall we say after this? for we have forsaken thy *commandments*" (emphasis added).

Notice the act was considered a violation of God's Commandments, an abomination. Why is racial integration a violation of God's Law? Because it destroys God's Covenant people and in the case of other races, it perverts what he created and called "good."

Chapter 10:3 states Israel corrected the problem: "Now therefore let us make a covenant with our God to put away all the wives, and such as are born of them, according to the counsel of my Lord, and of those that tremble at the *commandment* of our God; and let it be done *according to the law.*"

Here are a few more references to ponder:

- Genesis 6:4–5;
- Leviticus 21:14–15;
- Numbers 36:8;
- Deuteronomy 7:3;
- Deuteronomy 17:15;
- Judges 3:5–8;
- Nehemiah chapters 9 and 10.

A common problem that parallels the sin of interracial marriage and usually precedes it, is simply cohabiting, with those not of your race (multicultural society). The BIG problem is being led astray to follow other gods (Deuteronomy 7:4). This is very evident today.

Social engineers have been and will continue to be unsuccessful in amalgamating the various cultures. One of two things happens:

1. Natural segregation occurs—the black side of town, the oriental side, the Hispanic section and the white neighborhoods, etc. Think about it. It happens. Or,

2. The people of a city give up trying to be who they really are and adopt an artificial culture that borrows from each other until no one has an identity, a religion, a history, or a future for that matter. This ends in racial strife, not love and harmony. Just read the daily headlines.

The social engineers don't care about anyone's culture except the artificial one they hope to create—the UN person who worships the earth and obeys the master (New World Order government). Their only fear is people who will obey God's law!

I've mentioned the systematic and planned extermination of the white race (and others) but what of the attack upon the national and political spheres in their genocidal plan? The national identity of America is nearly invisible. The General Agreement on Tariffs and Trade (GATT) and the North American Free Trade Agreement (NAFTA) are two of the most recent blows and soon to follow, "global money" (debt). As the Master-Card commercial arrogantly states, "MasterCard: it's the future of money." With the elimination of nations comes the elimination of racial identity. It's a hand and glove thing.

A political genocide has already been accomplished. We all know global-government/politics has arrived in Babylon. To survive the political realm relies upon the spiritual wellness of a people—need I say more?

Once God's ambassadors are physically destroyed either by aborticide, or interracial genocide the spirit goes too! If it weren't for the spiritual connection, God's enemies wouldn't bother trying to destroy Israel as a race. No holy seed means no link to Yahweh.

I'm not trying to paint you a hopeless picture here. This war isn't over yet. There remains a remnant of people Yahweh plans to save in order to accomplish His will. I believe they are alive now and doing the right thing. More are to be born, no doubt. My purpose in this short commentary is to plant more seeds of understanding which will grow into trees of resistance for the destroyers.

They hate it when we do that because truth is so very hard to kill once it has landed on fertile ground. You may not see the urgency or appreciate the need to keep Yahweh's holy seed alive but you will. Hopefully *before* you or someone you know becomes involved in a very difficult situation, because destroying your offspring by interracial genocide is just as irreversible as aborting them—and carries the same judgment.

Praise Yahweh for the saving grace of YeHoshua!

7

The Bible Does Not Prohibit Interracial Marriage

Wesley Webster

Wesley Webster is a writer and a minister in the Worldwide Church of God, an international Christian church based in Pasadena, California.

Those who cite biblical passages to prove that God prohibits interracial marriage are misinterpreting scripture. The passages often cited forbid marriage between those of different faiths, not different races. Many prominent figures in the Bible, among them Moses and David, were married to women of different races. Other important figures of the Bible, including Solomon and Jesus, were of racially mixed ancestry. Racist thinking was so firmly woven into the American consciousness during the Jim Crow period of American history that it led many Christians to interpret the Bible through a haze of racial prejudice.

"Don't believe me, believe your Bible!" This is the greatest and most important legacy of Herbert W. Armstrong. When we veer away from the scriptures with our own private interpretation or speculation we easily go astray and offend. Formerly, the Worldwide Church of God [WCG] had a policy forbidding interracial dating and marriage. *Was this policy biblical?* Should we have such a policy in God's Church today?

In this paper we will see that an anti-miscegenation policy cannot be supported by scripture. Our past policy was not based on the Word of God. Therefore, we should not have such a policy in God's Church today.

We will also see that the policy to forbid interracial dating and marriage caused great offense in the past because it reflected the racism of America rather than the truth of God's Word. The aim of this paper is not to encourage interracial marriage, but simply to refute a policy that was not based on the Bible. As God's Church, we must strive to ensure that the Word of God is the foundation of our policy and doctrine and not the ideas, speculation, culture, or racism of men.

I remember how racism in the Worldwide Church of God offended my brother over 15 years ago when he attended services for the first, last

Reprinted from Wesley Webster, "Does God's Word Forbid Interracial Marriage?" web article at http://biblestudy.org/basicart/interace.html, by permission of the publisher.

and only time. I was new in the Church myself. I had just started attending. Filled with zeal and enthusiasm for the truth, I invited my brother to services so he could see for himself that we were a Church that stuck to the Bible.

Unfortunately, that Sabbath we had a taped sermon from headquarters given by Mr. Armstrong. Please understand, my aim here is not to attack Herbert Armstrong, but to illustrate how the misuse of scripture can offend. Mr. Armstrong made a point in his sermon of stating that Adam was white. This is repeated in *The Mystery of the Ages*, p. 148, "It is evident that Adam and Eve were created white. God's chosen nation Israel was white. Jesus was white. But it is a *fair* (emphasis added) conjecture that in mother Eve were created ovaries containing the yellow and black genes. . . ." Mr. Armstrong states emphatically that Adam was white without any proof, but is much less emphatic in stating that the other races came from Adam. The skin color of Israel and of Jesus is inconsequential to the skin color of Adam. We cannot claim that Adam was white because Abraham was white, or because Jesus was white. To do so is to make the Bible say something it clearly does not say.

Rather, the Bible indicates that Adam was the color of lentils—*reddish brown*. According to the *Hebrew-Greek Key Study Bible*, the name Adam means "reddish brown." The *Theological Wordbook of the Old Testament* (TWOT) shows that the name "Adam" comes from the root word, "adam" {aw-dam′}, *Strong's* #119, meaning "red." The color of "adam" is further substantiated by Genesis 25:30, where a derivative of this word is used to describe the lentil soup or pottage that Esau desired. If you look for lentils in the store, you will find that there are two types of lentils—a reddish brown lentil and a yellow lentil. According to the *Microsoft Encarta Electronic Encyclopedia*, "The fruit is a pod containing lens-shaped seeds, also called lentils, of which two varieties—small brown ones and larger yellow ones—are cultivated for table use." ("Lentil," Microsoft® Encarta. Copyright ©1994 Microsoft Corporation. Copyright ©1994 Funk & Wagnall's Corporation.) According to *Smith's Bible Dictionary*, under the heading, "Lentils," "Red pottage is made of the red lentil."

An anti-miscegenation policy cannot be supported by scripture.

This proves that Adam had a reddish brown complexion. Some translators have incorrectly substituted the word "ruddy" as a possible definition of the word "Adam." However, as we have seen, the word "adam" means "reddish brown." Lentils are not ruddy. No use of the word in the Bible supports "ruddy" as a definition of "adam." Every use of the word in the Bible is consistent with the color of lentils today—"reddish brown."

Mr. Armstrong's comments, therefore, were not based on the scriptures and deeply offended many black people in the Union, New Jersey, congregation, including my brother. Though I realized the comments about Adam's race were unfounded, I was willing to overlook this variance from the truth. Sadly, however, others, including my brother, were not able to look beyond this issue.

I cite this incident simply to illustrate that the greatest necessity for God's Church is to stick to the truth. When we stick to exactly what the Bible says, we won't offend. God warns us to be careful in Luke 17:1 saying, "It is impossible but that offenses will come: but woe unto him, through whom they come! It were better for him that a millstone were hanged about his neck, and he cast into the sea, than that he should offend one of these little ones."

Does the Bible forbid interracial or interreligious marriage?

God's message for his people is consistent from the beginning right to the end. God's way doesn't change back and forth. Let's notice now from the scripture that what God forbids in His Word is not the marrying of people of different racial lineage, *but interreligious marriage.*

Let's begin with Exodus 34:10–16:

> And he said, Behold, I make a covenant: before all thy people I will do marvels . . . behold, I drive out before thee the Amorite, and the Canaanite, and the Hittite, and the Perizzite, and the Hivite, and the Jebusite. Take heed to thyself, lest thou make a covenant with the inhabitants of the land whither thou goest, lest it be for a snare in the midst of thee: But ye shall destroy their altars, break their images, and cut down their groves: For thou shalt worship no other god: for the LORD, whose name is Jealous, is a jealous God; Lest thou make a covenant with the inhabitants of the land, and they go a whoring after their gods, and do sacrifice unto their gods, and one call thee, and thou eat of his sacrifice; And thou take of their daughters unto thy sons, and their daughters go a whoring after their gods, and make thy sons go a whoring after their gods.

Here we see God forbidding the Israelites from marrying people of the nations around them. The question we need to examine closely is why? *Was the prohibition based on race (especially as used in the sense of skin color) or on religion?*

From these verses we can clearly see that God's concern was that marrying outside the "Church" (Israel was the Church of the Old Testament) would cause Israel to turn away from God. The command is similar to what we read in the New Testament in 2 Corinthians 6:14, "Be ye not unequally yoked together with unbelievers . . .", and 1 Corinthians 7:39, "The wife is bound by the law as long as her husband liveth; but if her husband be dead, *she is at liberty to be married to whom she will; only in the Lord.*" God gave the saints liberty to marry anyone in the Lord regardless of race or skin color. The issue was the same for the Church in the wilderness.

Notice similar instructions in Deuteronomy 7:1–6. "Neither shalt thou make marriages with them; thy daughter thou shalt not give unto his son, nor his daughter shalt thou take unto thy son. For they will turn away thy son from following me, that they may serve other gods: so will the anger of the LORD be kindled against you, and destroy thee suddenly"(v. 3–4). The problem here was clearly that marrying outside the

"Church" would cause Israel to turn away from the true worship of the true God. Other scriptures that illustrate this truth are Joshua 23:6–13; Ezra 9:1–2, 10–14.

Now some would agree that the "main" issue had to do with religion, but would still hold on to the idea that race was also included. Let's now notice God's ruling on race, once religion is taken care of. Exodus 12:37–38 shows us that when Israel left Egypt, a mixed multitude went up with them. In Verse 43 God then explains that a stranger may not eat of the Passover. For a stranger to eat the Passover, he had to be circumcised (symbolic of spiritual conversion—see Romans 2:28–29). Once a stranger was circumcised, the scripture says "he shall be as one that is born in the land. . . . One law shall be to him that is home born and unto the stranger that sojourneth among you" (vv. 48–49).

If a stranger becomes *"as one that is born in the land"* then it would no longer be wrong for this stranger to marry an Israelite, or for an Israelite to marry him/her because they both at that point would be in the "Church." Thus we see that scripture forbids interreligious, not interracial marriage. The theory used in the WCG was that Noah's three sons married women of three different races in order to perpetuate the races after the flood. Without taking time to debate this issue, which in itself proves unfounded, the WCG therefore seemed to suggest that one must not cross the three major strains in marriage. Yet, scripture simply does not support this view. Rather, God's Word tells us we are all of one blood (Acts 17:26); we are all the descendants of Adam and Eve (Gen. 3:20); and we are all the descendants of Noah. We are in one sense, therefore, all of one race (family). If we trace our roots back, why stop at the sons of Noah for the purpose of marriage? What scripture indicates that we should stop there? The absence of a scriptural command on this delineation makes it clear such a policy is unscriptural.

Notice Israel was plagued for committing whoredom with Midianites—descendants of Abraham (Gen. 25:14). Solomon was rebuked for marrying, among others, Moabites, Ammonites, Edomites—all descendants of Shem (Genesis 19:36–38; Gen. 36). In both cases the problem was clearly that these strange wives led the Israelites away from the true worship of the true God. The problem was interreligious marriage, not interracial marriage.

Yet, on the other hand, Moses married a Midianite woman in Exodus 2:15–21 with no condemnation from God. The condemnation came from Miriam and Aaron and God was angry with them (Numbers 12:1–9). Nowhere in the Bible do we read of God correcting Moses for the wife he chose—even though she was black. Her skin color is proved by a comparative analysis of scripture which indicates that Jethro and Zipporah were black. Zipporah was identified as an Ethiopian woman in Numbers 12:1, Hebrew, "Cushite." Habakkuk 3:7 shows Cushan was an archaic term for the Midianites (see *New Bible Dictionary* p. 257). Jethro was also considered a Kenite in Judges 1:16. Zipporah was accepted by God because her religion was not wrong. Her father, Jethro, worshipped the true God (Exodus 18:10–27).

We see later that Boaz was the son of Rahab, the harlot, a Canaanite woman from Jericho. Rahab was accepted by God and allowed to marry an Israelite because she became a member of the "Church"—she accepted the religion of Israel (Hebrews 11:31). Boaz married Ruth, a Moabite. This was allowed because she accepted the true God. All of these historical facts show that Jesus' ancestry included *Gentiles* (Matthew 1:5; Luke 4:32). One should also note that Solomon was the son of Bathsheba, "daughter of Sheba" (Genesis 10:7) a descendant of Cush (remember Solomon later met with the Queen of Sheba, 1 Kings 10:1). Bathsheba, Solomon's mother, was also the former wife of Uriah the Hittite. Yet David was never criticized for marrying outside of his race. His sin was the sin of adultery. The marriage was later blessed by God rather than condemned, and the offspring of the interracial marriage was chosen by God to be the King of Israel, the wisest king of all time.

Misunderstood scriptures

Obviously, what God's word prohibits is interreligious marriage, not interracial marriage. Some would say at this point, *"What about the fact that Isaac and Jacob were instructed to marry their relatives* (Gen. 24:3–4; 28:1)?" Since the Israelites, as previously seen, were commanded not to marry relatives who were not "circumcised" or part of the Church, we realize the issue was not race but religion.

Some assume Abraham's motive for wanting Isaac to marry among his relatives was a desire to maintain racial purity. However, this cannot be proved in the scriptures. A more likely reason can be seen when we look at the example of Lot. Righteous Lot, Abraham's nephew, had children before Abraham did. Abraham learned from Lot's mistakes. When God destroyed Sodom and Gomorrah, Lot's sons-in-law would not leave the city, even though they were given the opportunity to do so. The problem was that they did not know the true God. They were not in the "Church" and were most likely steeped in pagan religion.

Abraham must have contemplated the problem of finding a wife for his son that would not be too heavily influenced by pagan religion. Accordingly, he considered it wiser to choose a wife from his relatives where he knew the Pagan influence was not very strong. One certainly cannot deduce or prove that Abraham's motive was race or racial purity. Therefore, one should not use Abraham's decision in choosing a wife for his son as the basis for a church policy to forbid interracial marriage.

Another misunderstood scripture is found in Genesis 6:9 where it says, ". . . Noah was a just man and perfect in his generations and Noah walked with God." Some believe the phrase, "perfect in his generations," means Noah was racially pure. This view is found in the *Companion Bible*. This was also the view of Herbert W. Armstrong. In the *Mystery of the Ages*, p. 148 we read, ". . . Noah, only, was unblemished or perfect in his generations—his ancestry. He was of the original white strain." However, a close look at the preceding verses shows conclusively that this view could not be correct.

Methuselah lived 187 years before he begat Lamech, and after that he lived another 782 years for a total of 969 years. When Lamech was 182 he begat Noah. Based on the scriptures (Gen. 5:25–32), at the time of Noah's birth, Methusaleh was 369 years old. Gen. 7:11 shows that Noah was 600 years old when he entered the Ark (600 + 369 = 969). Thus the flood came at the same time Methusaleh died. Yet, Noah was building the Ark and preaching righteousness for 120 years before the flood came, during

righteousness, or for the uprightness of thine heart, dost thou go to possess their land: but for the wickedness of these nations the LORD thy God doth drive them out from before thee, and that he may perform the word which the LORD sware unto thy fathers, Abraham, Isaac, and Jacob. Understand therefore, that the LORD thy God giveth thee not this good land to possess it for thy righteousness; for thou art a stiffnecked people."

It should be obvious from these verses that God did not choose Israel due to any superior heredity or righteousness on their part. He chose them according to the promise he made to Abraham, and God blessed Abraham because Abraham obeyed him, not because he was white (Gen. 26:5).

Flawed policy bears evil fruit

In Matthew 7:16–20 we are told to know a true minister by his fruits. We can also judge policies by their fruits. A good policy will not bear evil fruit. Let's notice that the policy forbidding interracial marriage in the WCG did bear evil fruit in the past.

First of all, the policy led to disastrous conclusions. I can remember a very unfortunate experience that I once had when I was being trained in the Ministry in 1987. The Assistant Pastor had me assist him in visiting a new contact and prospective member. The young lady was of mixed parentage. Her mother was white, and her father was black. She was very light in complexion, but her brother was very dark. Before inviting her to Church, the Assistant Pastor had to inform her that we did not allow interracial dating and marriage in the Church. We had no clear scriptures to support our point. However, the minister went on to explain that since she was not clearly in either racial group, she would have to decide before attending services which race (skin color) she would date. Her decision once approved would be final and lifelong. For approval she was required to write an essay explaining her decision which was to be sent to Pasadena along with a photograph, before a final decision could be made.

Why should ministers have the right to decide who she could date? On what grounds did the ministry exercise such authority over people's lives?

God's Word does not lead the ministry to control every aspect of people's lives. We should teach and preach the Word. When we go beyond the Bible we overstep the authority God has given us.

That we involved ourselves in such a ludicrous practice is shameful and presumptuous, and clearly contrary to the love of Almighty God. This was certainly a practice that could absolutely DESTROY one of God's little ones.

I'll always remember the day that I found out that I was accepted to go to Ambassador College. I'll always remember because the Pastor was instructed to inform me and make sure that I understood interracial dating at Ambassador was strictly forbidden. White males were not subjected to this questioning. This was definitely a form of racial discrimination and reflected the racist view that black men are desperately desirous of white women. These views are a carry over from the slavery and Jim Crow periods of the United States' history.

Another illustration of how racist the policy actually was is illustrated in the fact that what we actually prohibited in the Church was marriage across the lines of skin color, not interracial marriage (where race is understood as family as opposed to skin color). The policy was not enforced to forbid an Italian from marrying an Anglo-Saxon, so long as the skin color for each party was white. Yet such a marriage in some cases may be more interracial than a marriage of a white person and a black person depending on family lineage (as in the case of a black person—skin color—who has a white Anglo-Saxon parent and a black parent, marrying a white Anglo-Saxon).

The point of all of this is simply to show that our past policy lacked understanding. It was flawed biblically. It was offensive socially.

Origins of this racist policy

Where did this policy come from?

The policy came from the racist thinking of America. The view many white Americans held of black people was intimated in the *Dred Scott vs. Sandford* Supreme Court Decision in 1857. Chief Justice Roger B. Taney wrote the main opinion of the court. He said that the black race was "viewed as part of an inferior order, possessing no rights that the white race was obligated to respect. Blacks were deemed completely unfit to associate politically and socially with whites, and therefore, enslavement for their own benefit was viewed as lawful and justifiable" (*A Guide to American Law*, Vol. 4, 1984, p. 190).

The Jim Crow period of U.S. history, 1863–1953, perpetuated racist views in America, and through a caste system embedded racism into the very fabric of American thinking. Many white Americans held racist views of blacks without giving it much thought. One of the great fears instilled in the minds of many white Americans was the fear of racial amalgamation. Hence, it was generally viewed that the danger of miscegenation necessitated segregation and discrimination in nearly all spheres of life. Jim Crow thinking led to segregation and discrimination in recreation, in religious services (note: this took place in the WCG, even in States where Jim Crow laws were not even in force), in education (when Ambassador first got going, blacks were not allowed), before the law, in politics, in housing, in stores and in bread winning.

The past WCG policy on interracial marriage was no more than an extension of America's racist views. Racism had infiltrated many aspects of American life in order to justify the inhumane treatment of black people during the Slave period and beyond. Many intellectual and religious leaders supported slavery before the civil war and manipulated facts of science and even scripture to perpetuate their views.

However, at this time, we are in a position to formulate policy in the Church of God free from the racist viewpoint. We should therefore base our policy on scripture, and scripture alone. *Since the scriptures do not forbid interracial marriage, we must not forbid interracial marriage.*

By not forbidding interracial marriage, we are in no way implying that we encourage miscegenation. We are simply letting everyone decide for themselves based on their individual circumstances. As in any major decision, those seeking to be married should seek wise and abundant counsel (Prov. 11:14). Those contemplating marriage should take into consideration the feelings of their families, and the impact their decisions will have on those around them and on their progeny within the framework of the society.

8

Interracial Dating Among Teenagers Is Increasing

Karen S. Peterson

Karen S. Peterson is a contributor to USA Today.

According to a *USA Today* survey, 57 percent of teenagers in America have dated someone of a different racial background. Another 30 percent indicated that they would consider dating someone of a different ethnic background. A rise in immigration, which increases the amount of contact that teens have with people of different racial backgrounds, has been partly attributed to the rise in interracial dating. Also, many of today's parents have more liberal attitudes toward interracial dating as a result of growing up during the civil rights era. The rise in interracial dating among teenagers does not mean that racism is no longer a problem in America, but it is an encouraging sign of future race relations.

A s Americans struggle with racially charged issues from affirmative action to record-breaking immigration, high school students have started a quiet revolution that could signal a shift in the way the nation will come to look at race.

According to a 1997 *USA Today*/Gallup Poll of teenagers across the country, 57% who go out on dates say they've been out with someone of another race or ethnic group—whether white, black, Hispanic or Asian.

The poll also finds that some racial barriers remain, particularly between white and black teens. But experts who have explored the dynamics of the nation's growing multiculturalism believe many teens are on the leading edge of cultural change, looking at race in a way that seemed inconceivable just two decades ago.

"For a lack of a better term, there is a kind of de-racialization of American society hinted at in these statistics," says Elijah Anderson, an ethnographer at the University of Pennsylvania and author of *Streetwise*.

"You do have to be cautious, but I can see implications for interracial bonding in the future, implications for the workplace, for government," Anderson says.

Reprinted from Karen S. Peterson, "Interracial Dating: For Today's Teens, Race 'Not an Issue Anymore,'" *USA Today*, November 3, 1997, with permission. Copyright 1997, USA TODAY.

When Gallup last asked teens about interracial dating, in 1980, just 17% said they had dated someone of another race, though Hispanics were not specifically included in that count.

The results of the new poll, conducted Oct. 13–20, 1997 of 602 teens, reflect the ubiquity of interracial dating today—a trend strongly supported by anecdotal evidence gleaned from dozens of interviews across the country with teachers, school counselors, principals, parents and students.

"The very fact this many teen-agers are willing to say they have dated interracially is, I think, a big shift," says Ellis Cose, author of *Color-Blind: Seeing Beyond Race in a Race-Obsessed World.*

Increased contact with other races

In general, those interviewed say interracial dating has become far more common in part because heavy immigration of Hispanics and Asians has increased chances of meeting people from other racial and ethnic groups. Minority enrollment in public schools nationally is a record 35%, up from 24% in 1976.

They also credit increasing acceptance and frequency of interracial marriage: There were nearly 1.3 million married interracial couples in 1994, the Census Bureau reported, four times the number in 1970.

Although experts may view the teens' behavior at the vanguard of social change, the teens say it's no big deal.

"I think people are getting used to growing up with different races, and you feel a lot more comfortable now," says Vertrice Duke, 17, a student at Meadowcreek High, a racially diverse school in the Atlanta suburb of Norcross. "It's not like it is a color thing anymore. You have been with different races all your life." Vertrice, who is black, dates a Hispanic.

Angela McMillan, 16, and Eddie Untachantr, 16, are another Meadowcreek couple. Angela does not care that she is white and Eddie is Asian-American.

She dates Eddie for the reasons teens always date each other, she says: his "looks, his style, the way he dances. He plays soccer and so do I. We have a lot in common."

The poll supports those views. Many teens see "interracial dating" as just "dating":

- While 57% of teens who date say they have gone out with someone of another race or ethnic group, another 30% say they would have no objection to doing so.
- Dating with Hispanics accounts for a sizeable portion of interracial daters. But even removing Hispanics from the results, 31% of teens who date have done so interracially—almost twice the percentage found in the 1980 poll.
- In most cases, parents aren't an obstacle. A separate *USA Today*/Gallup Poll found 62% of parents of teens say they would be "totally fine" if their children dated interracially.

That does not surprise Reynolds Farley of New York's Russell Sage Foundation, which sponsors social science research. "The parents of these teens would be in their late 30s and early 40s," he says. "They will have experienced some of the liberal attitudes from the civil rights revolution."

- Virtually all teens (97%) say they or other teens date interracially because they "find the person attractive." Other frequent reasons include curiosity (75%); "trying to be different" (54%); and to rebel against their parents (47%).

- Interracial dating is much more likely to take place in suburbs (64%) and cities (64%) than in the nation's predominately white rural areas (40%).
- Thirteen percent say they will never cross racial lines.

This is not to say that all teens are dating across racial or ethnic lines, or that they want to.

Although the poll shows overwhelming acceptance of the practice, it also finds 43% of teens who date haven't dated interracially and 13% who say they never would.

Those teens report any number of reasons to pollsters, most sounding the familiar themes of racial division: "I've been raised that it wasn't right;" "You should stick with people of your own kind;" "Because you receive so much grief from society and it's not worth it;" "I wouldn't want to marry them."

When there are objections from teen-agers or parents to interracial dating, they show up most strongly in relationships with blacks, the poll found:

- Seventeen percent of white teens who date have gone out with a black. That's almost the same percentage who have dated an Asian, even though there are four times as many blacks as Asians in the United States.
- Forty-four percent of black teens who date have dated a white. That means blacks are almost as likely to date a Hispanic as a white, though whites vastly outnumber Hispanics.
- Black-white dating is most likely to cause teens trouble with other teens of their own race: 24% said whites would have a problem with a white teen dating a black; 23% said blacks would have a problem with a black teen dating a white. Just 8% say Asians would be troubled by an Asian teen dating a white.
- Finally, 35% of non-black teens who haven't dated interracially say their parents would object if they dated a black teen, compared with 20% whose parents would object to a white, Hispanic or Asian.

"That racial barrier is still the strongest," says University of Florida sociology professor Joe Feagin, who has researched race relations 31 years. "Blacks who date whites will get negative comments from their community. White parents feel that only over their dead bodies will their child ever date a black."

Mary Broadhurst also finds resistance. The past president of the Georgia School Counselors Association, Broadhurst says, "I have observed that black parents on the whole—and the white parents—don't want their kids dating" each other.

The problems with interracial dating

The teen-agers see problems, too. Vertrice Duke says her black friends want to make sure her boyfriend is known as Hispanic, not white. Dating a white boy would not be acceptable to them. "But everybody's cool about it now, because it's like, 'Oh, he's Spanish. He's not white,'" she says.

Thuy Hoang, 17, an Asian-American at Meadowcreek, dates white student Chris Brown, 18. They have no trouble, she says, though others might. "A lot of people don't look at me and Chris as being interracial," she says. "If you see a black person with a white person, they think that is interracial."

"The trend is growing very, very fast"

Part of the reason for such hostility is the continuation of the "color hierarchy" that teens learn at home, says Larry Hajime Shinagawa, chair of the department of American Multicultural Studies at Sonoma State University. "Any Asian daughter knows if she can't marry another Asian-American, her parents might tolerate a white person," he says.

Lydia Rosado, of the Committee for Hispanic Children and Families in New York, works with children of Spanish-speaking cultures. She has counseled many teenage girls whose parents "want them to date someone lighter in skin, not darker. Skin color is still a problem."

The teens here at Meadowcreek acknowledge they sometimes get flak—from peers and parents.

Shawn Boykin, 17, who is black, says black girls have hassled him for dating a white. "I just say, 'You only date black guys? So you just like to have the same cereal every morning?' and I feel I get the best of them."

And Shawn's girlfriend, Dawn Haney, 19, says she "spent a lot of nights crying, talking to my dad" before he agreed to Shawn's coming to their house.

Eddie Untachantr has felt some pressure. "I have been called a sell-out because a lot of the Asians at this school like to hang out just with each other," he says. "When they see me with a white girl, they feel like I'm singling myself out."

The very fact this many teen-agers are willing to say they have dated interracially is . . . a big shift.

But for the most part at Meadowcreek, teens say, the problems are small. Its 2,035 students attend one of the most diverse high schools in Georgia, with 34% whites, 29% blacks, 21% Asian-Americans, 14% Hispanics and 2% of other races.

"Our students pretty much choose their friends based on who they are, not their color," principal Patrick Mahon says.

As psychologist and author Brenda Wade puts it, even Disney has noticed the interracial dating trend.

Pocahontas is "an interracial dating story in a cartoon for children," she says. And Sunday's television remake of *Cinderella* starred the black pop singer Brandy, saved by a Philippine-born Prince Charming. The two productions show the dating phenomenon "has penetrated to the core of our culture," Wade says. "The trend is growing very, very fast."

It's being noticed.

In Los Angeles, says David Hayes-Bautista, director of the Center for the Study of Latino Health at UCLA's School of Medicine, "the phenomenon is going younger. . . . My daughter just turned 15 and among her and her friends, this is not even an issue anymore."

On the other side of the country, family therapist Kenneth Hardy each year asks his incoming marriage and family class at Syracuse University how many have been involved in interracial relationships. "The numbers go up each year. This past year, in a class of 200 students, about 40% said yes."

The question then becomes, where does it lead?

The changing face of America

In interviews, some experts go so far as to suggest the new poll findings, combined with studies showing greater acceptance of interracial marriage, portend literally a changing face for America's future. They project a multiracial nation symbolized by golfer Tiger Woods' self-proclaimed "Cablinasian" (Caucasian-black-American Indian-Asian) heritage.

"The more teen-agers date, the greater the likelihood they might marry," says Zhenchao Qian, a sociologist at Arizona State University. "We do see a great increase in interracial marriage in the last 20 years."

But many say linking teen dating and marriage may be getting ahead of the game.

"It's not like it is a color thing anymore. You have been with different races all your life."

Shinagawa says teens who date interracially in high school often prefer their own race later. "Many times they become politicized in college and rediscover their ethnic and racial identity," he says.

In fact, some experts note simultaneous trends: increasing racial hostility on college campuses and increasing collegial racial interaction in high school.

Parents, too, exert influence. And while many might not object to interracial dating, marriage could be another story.

Meadowcreek parent Doug Brown has no qualms about his son, Chris, dating an Asian-American. But he would worry about "serious decisions, permanent commitments." A major concern is religious differences. Chris, he says, is "pretty serious about his Church of God background. Something would have to give."

Charlie Moshell is the father of John Moshell, 18, who is white and dates Kate Llaga, 17, an Asian American at Meadowcreek. "I put rules down," his father says. "'These are the things you cannot do: interracial dating, drugs, homosexuality, orange hair or trouble with the law.'"

With interracial dating, Charlie Moshell worried about "culture clashes, complications for future offspring, things like that."

Although he changed his mind about John dating Kate, "I have cautioned him about problems getting married," Moshell says. But "race is not an issue now."

As for the teens themselves, many say they have enough trouble getting their act together for today, much less planning years into the future.

Who dates interracially?

Have dated someone of another race
- All 57%
- Whites 47%
- Blacks 60%
- Hispanics 90%

Have not, but would consider it
- All 30%
- Whites 36%
- Blacks 28%
- Hispanics 9%

Would not consider it
- All 13%
- Whites 17%
- Blacks 12%
- Hispanics 1%

Based on 496 teens who have dated.

9

Interracial Relationships Can Be Difficult to Accept

Gloria Wade-Gayles

Gloria Wade-Gayles is a professor of English and women's studies at Spelman College. She is the author of Rooted Against the Wind, *from which this viewpoint is excerpted.*

Black women face considerable difficulty overcoming their hostile feelings toward black men who marry white women. These relationships inspire feelings of abandonment and shame in African American women. Many feel that by marrying white women, black men send the message that white is better, a message that causes many black women to question their self-worth. Black women must learn to let go of their anger toward interracial relationships. There are more important things that deserve their anger, such as poverty and racial injustice.

I remember in my high school and college years being proud of the black man in *Mod Squad*. He was so very hip, so very visible, so very much an equal in the trio that fought crime. "Day-O. Day-O. Daylight come and me wanna' go home." I would Calypso dance in front of the mirror to [Harry] Belafonte's scratchy voice singing melodiously. And like other black women, I was proud of Sidney Poitier, that ebony brother of tight smoothness, who was the first of the big stars. There was something in the way he walked, leaning down in his hips, in the way he read a script through his eyes, in the way his deep blackness spoke of a power that was mine to claim. I remember wanting the mellifluous voice that made James Earl Jones brilliant in any role—from "street" to Shakespearean. All married white women.

The pain we experience as black teenagers follows many of us into adulthood, and, if we are professional black women, it follows with a vengeance. As a colleague in an eastern school explained our situation, "Black men don't want us as mates because we are independent; white men, because we are black." We have to organize our own venting sessions. The only difference between us and black teenagers is the language we use,

Excerpted from *Rooted Against the Wind*, by Gloria Wade-Gayles. Copyright ©1996 by Gloria Wade-Gayles. Reprinted by permission of Beacon Press, Boston.

our attempt at some kind of analysis, and our refusal to mourn. Teenagers see an individual heartthrob; we see an entire championship basketball team: "Can you believe that every single black starter on the team has a white wife?" Teenagers know about athletes and entertainers; we know about politicians and scholars. Teenagers see faces; we see symbols that, in our opinion, spin the image of white women to the rhythm of symphonic chords. In our critique of *Jungle Fever,* for example, we see the carnival walk, the music, the cotton candy, the playful wrestling, which all precede sex between the black man and his white lover; and therefore we cannot miss seeing the very different symbols for the man and his black wife. The movie begins with them making such hard love—passion is what it is supposed to be—that the daughter asks, "Daddy, why were you hurting Mama?" Teenagers are so preoccupied with heartthrobs who marry "wrong" that they forget the men who marry "right." We don't. Adult black women all but cheer when we hear that a black male luminary is married to a black woman. Sadly, we do not discuss how the right-thinking brother treats his wife. What matters is that he *chose* one of us.

Choice

Choice is the key word in our reading of marriages between black women and white men and good treatment is our focus. The sister didn't do the choosing. She was *chosen.* Isn't that how it works in patriarchy? The man, not the woman, asks, "Will you marry me?" And didn't many of us in the Civil Rights movement, myself included, support the notion that marriages between black women and white men (unlike those between black men and white women) said more about the gains we thought we had achieved than the new laws which were never meant to be aggressively enforced? The men shook the very foundation of the system by legally marrying women the system saw as anybody's sexual property. We tended, therefore, to see white men and black women through a more accepting lens. Our logic might have been flawed, but the issue was never about logic in the first place.

What's more, our argument continued, black women are immune to the charge of disloyalty, having demonstrated down through the ages and in all circumstances unswerving, unshakable—and perhaps insane— devotion to black men. For us, there was no credence to the idea that black women who marry interracially suffer the affliction of their counterparts among black men, that is, a preference for white. Since women love so easily, and so well, often foolishly, for us, the choice is more than likely a matter of the heart. Case closed for black women married to white men because the number is comparatively minuscule. Trial in session for black men married to white women because there were, in our opinion, too many of them who went that way immediately after their success in white America.

A preference for white

The trial is still in session, and because of the nature of race relations in our nation, we are pounding an iron-heavy gavel. We think we can read these men without ever seeing lines in the palms of their hands. We believe we know them by the signs they wear, flashing neon and without apology. They are the men who date only white; who attend only predominantly, or so-called integrated, gatherings; who can't remember expressions, songs, places, or people from home; who make as few trips home as possible; who refer to black people as "they"; and who have a long list of what "black people/they" shouldn't say and how "black people/they" shouldn't act.

Black men don't want us as mates because we are independent; white men, because we are black.

But not always. Sometimes black men in interracial relationships are like the character Truman in Alice Walker's *Meridian*: "blacker than thou" and equipped with the rhetoric, the walk, and the haircut to prove as much. For them, everything good is black, or, more precisely, African. And what better good for the nation than black babies, and who other than black women can give the people, or them, those new soldiers/warriors?

But we believe we know them most certainly by a contempt they cannot conceal. It is in their body movements, their words, their eyes, and the odor of their perspiration when they are forced to be in close proximity with us.

Those we do not know personally who shape a steep mountain on the graph of interracial marriages—the entertainers, athletes, politicians, etcetera—we nevertheless judge. Regardless of the signs they wear, our verdict is the same: they marry white because they prefer white. It is a matter of the mind, not the heart. Isn't that what Frantz Fanon told us in *Black Skin, White Masks?* Never mind that Fanon was *not* an African-American and was *not* writing about our unique racial reality in these United States. We dig into a dung heap of Freudian analysis until we locate the phrase that says what we want to hear:

> *By loving me [the white woman] proves that I am worthy of white love. I am loved like a white man.*
> *I am a white man.*

We know about exceptions to this rule, but give them little time in our venting sessions. We say, "It's not like that with _____," or "They are in love, period," and we promise to fight any Ku-Kluxer or rabid black nationalist who attempts to disturb their hearth. But the second in which we acknowledge they exist is followed by an hour of venting. This seems to make good sense, for exceptions in any situation never represent the problem. They are precisely that: *exceptions.* They do not change the rule.

The pain of self-hatred

Nor do they change our history of pain as black women, or save us from the self-hatred that turns us into erupting volcanoes at the sight of a black man with a white woman. We see them, and we feel abandoned. We feel abandoned because we have been abandoned in so many ways, by so many people, and for so many centuries. We are the group of women furthest removed from the concept of beauty and femininity which invades almost every spot on the planet, and, as a result, we are taught not to like ourselves, or, as my student said, not to believe that we can ever do enough or be enough to be loved and desired. The truth is we experience a pain unique to us as a group when black men marry white women and even when they don't.

It is a pain our mothers knew and their mothers before them. A pain passed on from generation to generation because the circumstances that create the pain have remained unchanged generation after generation. It has become a part of us, this pain, finding its way to the placenta and to the amniotic waters in which we swim before birth. "From the moment we are born black and female," Audre Lorde writes, we are

> *Steeped in hatred—for our color, for our sex, for our effrontery in daring to presume we had a right to live. As children we absorbed that hatred, passed it through ourselves, and for the most part, we still live our lives outside of the recognition of what that hatred is and how it functions.*

We struggle to be whole in a society of "entrenched loathing and contempt for whatever is Black and female." I have been writing specifically about the pain heterosexual women feel when black men choose white women, but heterosexuals do not own this pain. Black lesbians experience it also, for in their world race choices or race rejections are evident in love relationships.

I look at my past participation in venting sessions with gratitude for the liberation I now experience, a liberation that was slow and gradual, and yet that seems to have happened overnight, as if while I slept someone or something cut the straps of the straightjacket that was stealing my breath and, miraculously, I awoke able to breathe with arms freed for embracing. It must have been a good spirit who knew the weight of anger had become too much for me, too much, and that I wanted to be done with it. Relieved of it. Freed from it. The truth is, I was carrying too much anger—anger over what integration did not mean for the masses of black people; anger over the deterioration of black schools; anger over battering and homicide of black women; anger over violence against our children, our elderly, and our young men; anger over the writing of books (by blacks no less) that lie about our character and misread the cause of our suffering; anger over misogynist lyrics; anger over . . . ANGER. It was a long list; it was a heavy weight which I had to lighten or lose my mind. The question was, What could I/should I remove? What was important and what was not important? What could I change and what couldn't I change? What should a former activist take on as a mission and not take on? What was my business and not my business? What could make a difference in the world?

Out of focus

The answer to those questions came with the clarity of a mockingbird singing from a rooftop in a North Carolina dawn, identifying herself and the place she has claimed as her own. I could see myself flying to a spiritually high place, identifying myself as a woman who loves herself, and claiming as my own a different place for struggle. Perched there, singing, I knew I would never again give my mind and my emotions over to something I could not change, did not have the right to change, and something that was not the cause of suffering in the world. I decided to remain focused in my anger, the better to be useful in a struggle for change, for the new justice we so desperately need. Anger over black men with white women, I sang, took me out of focus.

Adult black women all but cheer when we hear that a black male luminary is married to a black woman.

The percentage of black men marrying out of the race might be greater than the percentage of white men, but what are we talking about in terms of numbers? I began to ask myself. "Miniscule," I answered. There are twenty-plus million African-Americans (actually more, given tricks census plays) and I was sucking in all of that negativity because of a personal decision that a small group makes! The numbers don't add up to a million; at last count they constituted less than five percent of all black marriages. I talked to myself:

"Nonsense."
"No, it's not nonsense at all."
"Less than five percent. That's small."
"Not really. Actually, small is big for us."
"What do you mean?"
"The small number includes the big men. Men of influence."

Even so, I was quite simply weary of the weight of "the problem." I sang about going elsewhere with my anger. Anger, channeled creatively and used to galvanize us into constructive action, is an important emotion not to be wasted. In the spiritual place to which I was journeying, I wanted my anger to count, to stay on the high road of resistance, where it could target changes in the socioeconomic reality of my people rather than changes in colors worn at wedding ceremonies. I decided that interracial marriages did not deserve so precious an emotion.

Imprisoned by race

Weariness was one factor in my liberation; my love for children, another. How strange (and yet not so strange if I believe Spirit works in our lives) that when I was struggling with my liberation, interracial children became more visible than ever in grocery stores, shopping centers, and other public places. In almost all cases, their mothers were white. In the past, I would see them and think about the same old pattern: white mother, black father. Now I see the children and forget their parents, having decided that I cannot truly accept them if I question the union in which they were conceived. And the children I will never *not* accept. As if they are making a point, babies drop their pacifiers at my feet, toddlers bump into me, and at checkout counters, infants, propped in padded seats, face me rather than their white mothers. How innocent they are!

How unaware they are of the insanity in the world we have created. How necessary it is for us to stop talking about who married whom and receive the children without qualification into the circle of our embrace. Our failure to do so pushes them as teenagers into the quicksand of peer acceptance, forcing them to choose to be either black or white. Given this pressure, it is not surprising that they are sometimes the most strident voices of anger in the venting session and that their journal entries are often the most pained. That was the case with a student in the seminar on autobiography. She didn't "look" biracial (but, then, how do *they* always look?), but in a poignant autobiographical narrative, entitled "Trapped by Silence," she wrote about the pain of being the daughter of a white mother and a black father. Trapped in a nation imprisoned by race, she was uncomfortable with the "cotton-white" skin of her mother and obsessed with becoming black.

> *Everything my mother loved, I hated. Everything she did, I avoided. With everything she said, I disagreed. . . . How great a darkness that was! My only hope seemed to appear in places which glittered like pyrite. "The blacker, the better" seemed to be my theme. . . . I began worshipping black boys, the same boys I had avoided like liver and onions only a year before because they reminded me that I, too, was a part of their culture. "But now I am BLACK," I thought.*

What pain can be more consummate, I thought as I read her narrative, than rejection, no matter how brief, of the mother who births us.

The student wanted me to share her experiences in hopes that they would open the lens of our understanding to other dimensions of "the problem" and thereby make possible for other biracial children the acceptance of self she finally celebrates.

> *I had tried so hard for so long to be white, and then to be black, that I intentionally or foolishly forgot that I am both. After being accepted to Spelman College, I realized that I would have the opportunity to experience the world I had never known, and my mother would be the provider of that opportunity. . . . I anticipated my chance to be my white and black self. I began to close the chapter of my life replete with cultural confusion and open a chapter filled with acceptance of my complete self. I no longer felt I had to choose one or the other, so I embraced both as I gathered my stuff.*

A new list of concerns

A maternal woman (who is ready for grandchildren), I have always delighted in waving bye-bye or playing peek-a-boo with children I see in grocery stores and shopping malls, but recently it seems that biracial children are seeking me out for a hug; and ever since I read "Trapped by Silence," they seem to be in all the public places I find myself. They reach toward me, perhaps to test me. I give them what I give all children: my love. I am reminded, as I was not before my enlightenment, that the only difference between these children and my grandmother and probably my great-great-grandmother is that, unlike them, these children exist because of a union entered into willingly, for whatever the reason, and lived in the full light of day. That is what the student who wrote the poignant narrative came to understand: in the full light of day, her parents celebrated their coming together and her birth.

We see [black men with white women], and we feel abandoned.

At a different spiritual place, I made a new list of concerns that, working in coalition with others, I should address, have a moral obligation to address. Black men with white wives didn't make it on the list. I would be false to truth and, therefore, to my soul if I said I no longer believe that most black men with white wives have problems with themselves, with the race, and with black women. I will not lie. I believe many of them wear the aroma of disdain we can smell miles away. I believe that for most of them the choice is not a matter of the heart; but not knowing who in the group followed his heart (How *can* I know?), I have decided not to judge. Like a recovering alcoholic who is hooked all over again with one sip, I have written my own recovery program. It is composed of one step: remember how much lighter you feel without the weight of anger and the weight of judging.

10

Interracial Children Face Many Difficulties

Marta I. Cruz-Janzen

Marta I. Cruz-Janzen is an assistant professor in the department of secondary education at the Metropolitan State College of Denver. She is co-author of Educating Young Children in a Diverse Society.

Biracial children face considerable difficulties because society is obsessed with rigid racial boundaries. These boundaries exacerbate racial tension within and between different racial groups. Though biracial children are part of two cultures, they are often ostracized and rejected by both. If biracial children gain acceptance, it is usually as a result of rejecting half of their background. If these children are to have any hope of claiming their full identity, society must shed its rigid racial designations.

We live with a "box mentality." We sort and box people into racial categories set by rigid boundaries between groups. These boundaries exacerbate the tension within groups and between them. I am Latinegra. Both my parents are Puerto Rican; one black, the other, white. The U.S. has lumped all Latinos, from Latin America, North America, and Spain, together as "Hispanics," ignoring the vast cultural, economic, language, national, political, and racial diversity that exists within this classification. Growing up as biracial, between Puerto Rico and the mainland, acquainted me, at an early age, with racial prejudice rooted in all aspects of Latino and American culture.

Accordingly, multiracial Americans are pressured to fit neatly and quietly within one of four racial boxes, many of us getting tossed from box to box.

In 1993, an Hispanic reader from New Mexico wrote to *Hispanic* magazine, in response to earlier coverage of Latino major league baseball players which included black Latinos: "I would appreciate knowing how the writer arrived at the classification of apparent blacks as Hispanics? Does the fact that these men come from Spanish-speaking countries such as Puerto Rico or Cuba automatically give them the Hispanic designation?

Reprinted from Marta I. Cruz-Janzen, "It's Not Just Black and White: Who Are the Other 'Others'?" *Interrace*, Fall 1998, with permission.

History shows that Africans were transported to the Americas as slaves and took the names of their slave masters."

The resounding attitude among some Hispanics/Latinos is that I am not one of them because of my "one-drop" of "black blood."

Caught between two worlds

"Hispanics are from Spain," an Hispanic educator told me two years ago. "You are not Hispanic. You are black." In other words, "How dare *you* speak Spanish and claim to be one of us."

Although family and friends call me *triguena* (wheat-colored), I recall the cruel taunts of classmates, adults, and even teachers. I was repeatedly called *negativo* (photo negative) because while I resemble my mother, I am black and she is white. Being called *Perlina* was supposed to be a compliment. Perlina was a popular bleaching detergent with the picture of black children dressed in white on the label: I was a bleached black person. Due to my biracial heritage, I stood out among my classmates. They teased that I was *"una mosca en un vaso de leche"* (a fly in a glass of milk).

Growing up as biracial . . . acquainted me . . . with racial prejudice rooted in all aspects of Latino and American culture.

A high school teacher in New York advised me to identify as black because "that's how others will see you and that's how you will be treated, even by Latinos." Yet, there are Puerto Ricans and other Latinos who insist that I am *not* black. In fact, some scold me for being "too black" and advise me to be more Latina instead.

African Americans don't necessarily accept me either because I "don't understand or think like black folks." Ironically, they also tell me that I am ashamed of my black heritage by claiming to be Latina and speaking Spanish. They urge me to finally accept who I am. "Puerto Ricans are nothing but black folks in hiding."

Race is a political construct

My experience with others and how they perceive me is frustrating and painful; one that is common for an increasing number of multiracial Latinos, caught in the race wars that mar our country. Americans have a strong need to categorize and segregate—to sustain the white majority and oppress "weaker" minorities. While this is common to all human societies, color, race, and ethnicity in America have become uniquely political.

Our society designates multiracial individuals, although many are part white—some predominantly white—as "persons of color," at the same time making them undesirable to all parties because they do not unequivocally fit in the categorical box. Part-white multiracial Americans are pushed to identify with their communities of color where they are similarly not accepted. Multiracial persons with two "ethnic" parents are also rejected by both groups, though they are pushed to identify with the group of lower social status.

In addition to being denied full and equal membership into various groups, multiracial persons are forced to choose between groups.

A 26-year-old multiracial woman of Anglo-American and white Latino heritage recalls the rejection by her American white friends after being labeled Hispanic in high school: "I wasn't one of them. Suddenly, I was different." She recalls the frustration: "I didn't get along with this side and I didn't get along with that side. . . . No matter what I did somebody was always mad at me." To gain the acceptance of Latinos, she had to practically renounce her Anglo-American heritage. Furthermore, "I had to tell 'whitey' jokes," even ones directed toward her father.

Mainstream American society is obsessed with whiteness and the exclusion of anyone who is not of anglo descent. It has created a caste system whereby Anglo-Americans are elevated to the highest status relative to that of "others."

The historical objective of American citizenship is assimilation—the process whereby "minority" groups shed their ethnic heritage and ultimately adopt the standards established by the Anglo-American majority.

A young woman of Anglo-American and white Latino heritage expressed her fears: "I fit in [with whites] because of the way I look . . . I had to be white. I couldn't be Latino too." She knew that she would be "ostracized somehow" if she revealed her Latino heritage. Those who cannot blend in become "something else"—something *other* than white—which includes Spaniards and their descendants.

"Africa begins in the Pyrenees" is an European expression which clearly reflects disdain for both Africa and Spain. With a long history of interracial unions before they set sail for the Americas, Spaniards and Latinos are considered racially impure; unfitting for membership in the global white world.

Part-white multiracial Americans are pushed to identify with their communities of color where they are similarly not accepted.

African ancestry (as little as "one-drop") is perceived by whites and, in fact, most non-white groups as the bottommost on the racial pole. Newcomers to America learn this quickly and move as far away from any black likening as possible, physically and psychologically. Many black immigrants from around the world, including the darkest black Latinos, disavow any connection to African Americans.

The American culture myth

American culture has additionally promoted the myth that all Europeans share an un-ethnic "American culture." Ethnic issues become the concern of others and multicultural education, the study of "minorities." To be American and white is to be "normal." All others—the so-called minorities—are abnormal and un-American. A young woman, whose father is white Latino and whose mother is white American, stated her white fi-

SHELTON STATE LIBRARY

ancé's nervousness about her dual heritage and recounted a "huge argument" they had because he insisted that she was not biracial since she had blonde hair and blue eyes. "You are white," he concluded.

As an educator, and particularly an elementary school principal, I witnessed the acrimonious politics of ethnic and racial group membership and rejection played out at all school levels. For instance, a fourth grader, who was often in my office for verbal and physical aggression against both teachers and classmates, was, after several years, able to put into words his anguish. This son, of a Mexican American father and Anglo-American mother, hated his parents "for having me." In a predominantly Latino school, he was a social outcast, jeered by classmates, called a "white boy." His parents, especially his mother, were the objects of derisive jokes.

Social outcasts

A 26-year-old multiracial woman of white Latino and Native American parentage expressed similar anger. "Why did they [parents] have me? Didn't they think that this was going to be so hard? Who were they to decide my fate?"

A multiracial adult male whose mother is white Latino and whose father is Anglo-American recalled crying inconsolably at recess when he was young. "I would go off by myself in a corner and cry. I didn't have any friends. Nobody liked me." He wanted to be like everybody else. He reminds me of a second grader of Mexican American and African American parentage who would also cry and cry in my office unable to tell me why except she had no friends and nobody liked her either.

Persons of multiple ethnic and racial heritage no longer want to be invisible—accepted by none, condemned and rejected by all.

I can still hear the anguished cry of a beautiful multiracial middle school student of black Latino and white Latino ancestry who was called "ape man" and "jungle bunny" by her peers. She left for school one morning feeling on top of the world wearing a new outfit; her hair professionally styled for the first time. She thought her classmates would compliment her. Instead, they—especially Latino boys—insisted that no matter what she did to herself, she still looked like a monkey; she was still ugly. They threw water all over her new clothes and hair.

Another Mexican–African American recalls being rejected by her community. "I was looked down upon because I thought I was Mexican. They'd make fun of my hair, the thickness of my hair. They would call me nigger, black, and other names. The boys let me know that they didn't think I was attractive. The Mexican girls were really mean—evil. They were my friends but they would not allow me to be Mexican. They would always let me know that I wasn't like them—I wasn't Mexican."

A high school teenager of black Latino and white Latino parentage walked out of school and came home crying to tell her parents that she no longer wanted to return. That day a teacher in her predominantly white school taught that [all] black people had been brought to America as slaves. Her peers taunted her. They called her nigger, slave, pushed and shoved her, and ordered her around.

In a predominantly Latino middle school, a child of African American and Latino Indian ancestry was sent to the office for fighting at recess. During geography class her peers insisted that it was O.K. for whites to call blacks niggers because black people had named themselves that. There is a country [Niger] in Africa named after them, they insisted.

Racial hostility

Certainly not all multiracial Latinos are barraged with insults and objection. But very few escape the narrow-minded legacy of slavery and bigotry. My own child, then in middle school, pleaded that her Anglo-American father not attend a school program for fear that her black and Latino friends would see him. White students had rejected her, together with other black and Latino students. Her friends knew I was Latinegra but they did not know her father was white.

Ours is a culture that confers preferential treatment on lighter-skinned individuals, further pitting people of color against each other, within and between groups—and certainly within families. White attributes, such as long, straight hair, thin lips, and refined nose shapes, are more attractive and desirable. The coveting of whiteness also leads to resentment within and between "ethnic" groups. Indeed, lighter skin may be more desirable, but it is also equated with possessing the blood of the enemy. While trying to promote their own superiority, darker-skinned people resent their lighter-skinned members, especially those of multiracial heritage.

The mainstream school environment is often ethnically and racially hostile to students of color, but especially multiracial students who have no on-campus support system. Most of the antagonism and abuse of multiracial children occurs in the school environment. Furthermore, teachers and students alike insist that multiracial students identify exclusively with one group, primarily the group with the lowest social status. As a result, multiracial students are often harassed and rejected by all sides.

Self-identification is a human right

Though much debate continues to take place within some communities about the pros and cons of a multiracial category in the upcoming U.S. census, the fact is that this is not an exclusive "black and white" issue. Yet, the debate continues in almost complete disregard for the historical background of racism in the creation of racial and ethnic labels, and the fact that the rapidly growing multiracial population today is not solely of black and white backgrounds, but of various multicolored unions.

Persons of multiple ethnic and racial heritage no longer want to be invisible—accepted by none, condemned and rejected by all. Certainly, for the sake of our children, multiracial individuals must exist as valid members of humanity and demand inclusion, legitimacy, and recognition. Not until all Americans are granted the basic human right of self-identification in a diverse society will we shed our "box mentality" and break the shackles of psychological slavery that still bind us; the shackles that create bosses and servants, slave masters and slaves, and superior and inferior human beings. Only then will we be able to sit together at the American table as one.

11

Interracial Children Succeed in Life

Francis Wardle

Francis Wardle is the founder of the Center for the Study of Biracial Children and author of Tomorrow's Children, *published by the center.*

There are many reasons why biracial children often grow up to be very successful. According to research, parents of biracial children tend to be more independent and goal-oriented than parents of monoracial children, and these characteristics are often passed on to their children. Interracial parents also tend to be better educated than their monoracial counterparts, which means that they expect their children to succeed in school. Because they are raised in an atmosphere of high expectations and support, biracial children are capable of overcoming the limiting stereotypes that society places on them.

"All in all, they represent a rather successful group in this society." So said Dr. [Alvin] Poussaint in a 1985 article about biracial college students. R.C. Johnson, in an article on Asian/White biracial children in Hawaii, claims these children score very high on general knowledge IQ tests. Some studies suggest biracial adolescents have as high or higher self-esteem than single race adolescents. And the theory of hybrid vigor postulates that, through cross-gene pool breeding, biracial people are hardier and have greater genetic potential.

Great multiracial heroes like Frederick Douglass, W.E.B. Dubois, Langston Hughes, Josephine Baker, James Audubon, writer Velina Hasu Houston, Eartha Kitt, Lena Horne and the singers Mariah Carey, Lenny Kravitz, Sade and Paula Abdul certainly illustrate this success.

Most ethnic models and many ethnic actors are actually biracial or multiracial (Sonia Braga, Jennifer Beals, Naomi Campbell, Christy Turlington, etc.). And then there are athletes like Daley Thompson and Dan O'Brien, past world decathlon champions; skater Tai Babalonia, and Olympic gymnast Betty Okino. Numerous children in gifted and honors programs in our schools are biracial.

Reprinted from Francis Wardle, "Are Biracial Children Successful?" *Biracial Child*, Winter 1994, with permission.

It does seem, in relationship to the total number of biracial and multiracial people in this country, that products of mixed-race parentage are quite successful and often very beautiful.

Why?

There are many possible explanations. Johnson's Hawaii research also documents that women who crossed racial/ethnic lines to marry (Asian/White) were more independent than women who marry within a racial/ethnic group. Considering the societal, professional and family pressures against interracial marriage, it's logical to suppose people who marry interracially are independent, strong-willed and assertive. They are willing to buck the system for what they believe in. Surely these parents will raise self-willed, goal-oriented, independent children.

It does seem . . . that products of mixed-race parentage are quite successful and often very beautiful.

There is also research that shows interracially married partners tend to be better educated than people who marry within their racial/ethnic group. Clearly this means biracial children tend to grow up in educated families, and are expected to succeed in school.

Access to both cultures

Terry P. Wilson, in an article in the book, *Racially Mixed People in America*, discusses Native American/White people who were able to use their biracial heritage to access both cultures. This gave them an advantage. On many occasions they could negotiate the needs of their tribal people with White land owners, businessmen and politicians. Sometimes they used this advantage to better themselves. But they were also able to help their own people. So much so that many tribes changed their definition of "full blood" to enable these mixed-race Indians to participate in tribal politics.

Wilson says, "those who are comfortable half in the Indian world and half in the non-Indian world possess a third positive dimension stemming from biculturality that renders them 150% men."

Our children's access into two worlds, and the ability to feel comfortable in both, is a distinct advantage.

The parents

And then there's the observation that interracial parents are very conscientious. They're more picky about the schools their children attend. They are always at the school demanding the best for their children. They are involved in PTAs, homework, field trips, etc. They know the rest of the world wants them to fail as parents. And—by God—they are going to prove the rest of the world wrong!

This position is supported by research results on Asian American children. These children are by far more academically successful than any other group of children, including White; research shows their parents have high expectations, know their children must work hard to overcome their background, and require lots of parent support. Parents of Asian American children spend lots of time helping their children, monitoring the TV, and working with the school.

And these parents don't take a victim attitude: they believe that, with hard work, their children can succeed.

The research on Black and biracial children adopted by White families shows that transracially adopted children have as high, and sometimes higher, sense of ethnic pride and identity than do minority children raised in their biological homes, or in Black adoptive homes. This suggests the effort and commitment made by the White parents does have a positive impact. It also implies that conscientious interracial parents will have a positive impact on their children.

Interracial parents are very aware of the overall societal, professional and media biases against our families and children. We also know we must raise our children strong enough to withstand a history of negative writings, misguided scientific studies, and obnoxious characterizations of multiracial people in movies, novels and dramas.

Misconceptions

In a 1894 decision, a judge said, "the amalgamation of the races is not only unnatural, but is always productive of deplorable results . . . the offspring of these unnatural connections are generally sickly and effeminate, and they are inferior in physical development and strength, to the full blood of either race." Multiracial people were viewed as being weak physically, mentally, emotionally and morally, leading to early deaths and inability to reproduce, and eventually to group extinction (which is one reason many object to the word "mulatto", because a mule cannot reproduce). They were characterized as depressive, criminal, chronically confused and ruled by passion.

Our children's access into two worlds, and the ability to feel comfortable in both, is a distinct advantage.

Mixed-race women ("half-breed" Indians, Mexican mestizas, Eurasians and mulattas) were portrayed in books as sexually immoral, promiscuous, extremely passionate, and out of control.

Stonequist, a social scientist of the 1930s, called racial hybrids the most obvious type of marginal man. Much of today's academic community, including school officials, still support this belief.

Australia and the United States of America were originally made up of criminals, social and religious misfits, slaves, indentured servants, and natives whom civilized Europe viewed as primitive. These countries expended considerable individual and collective energy to overcome this negative history, and have advanced beyond their European ancestors.

In striving to overcome a negative history, and to rise above the current societal pressure, interracial parents, biracial children and multiracial people will succeed. Almost every interracial family I have met in my travels across this country have been very conscious of the hurdles they must overcome, and very committed to raise successful children.

This is the environmental argument.

Hybrid vigor

And then there is the biological argument: hybrid vigor. Most successful plants and animals in today's highly specialized agriculture are hybrids developed to increase yield and reduce vulnerability to diseases: Palomino and American Quarter horses, Brangus, Santa Gertruda and various Zebu cattle crosses, roses, tulips, trees, wheat, etc. The green revolution (dramatically increasing the yield of corn in developing countries) is the direct result of a hybrid. A rancher in Colorado has just sent mixed-breed cattle to Russia to replace the pure breed cows that cannot withstand the severe Russian winters.

The biological act of combining genes from two distinctive gene pools increases the health and strength of the resulting organism. With people it reduces the likelihood of genetically transmitted diseases and increases physical and mental possibilities.

And because interracial marriage maximizes these possibilities—both genotypically (the genes the person inherits) and phenotypically (the visual and physical result of those genes)—multiracial children will have new and different looks. This might explain the successes of multiracial fashion models and actors. The fashion world thrives on the novel, different and non-stereotypical images. Multiracial models are used a lot simply because they *cannot* be categorized as European, Asian, Hispanic, Native American or Black. And what's wrong with that?

When we consider our children are both the result of a caring, supportive and high expectation environment, and hybrid vigor, there is a temptation to claim they are, in fact, more successful and more beautiful than single race children. And for those of us (mostly parents) who are constantly told our children will fail this temptation is even greater.

Understandably people like Cynthia Nakashima, who in her article in *Racially Mixed People in America,* warn against this temptation. Part of her concern is that this position is based on the racist assumption that the White part of a biracial child's heritage is what makes them successful and beautiful, and the Asian part of a biracial person with Asian heritage makes them bright. Another reason is our memory of the tragic results of the Nazi concept of superior race.

In striving to overcome a negative history, and to rise above the current societal pressure...biracial children and multiracial people will succeed.

While we obviously must reject this position of superiority, it's disheartening to realize many who express this concern are quite comfortable suggesting our children are intellectually, physically and socially inferior to monoracial children, and that, for purely political reasons, any child with minority heritage must identify with their minority group. Surely, Hitler's insistence on a superior race was largely for political reasons.

We cannot afford to forget that the eugenics movement at the early part of this century included multiracial people among those to be eliminated.

Racism

As Nakashima points out, when we talk about people being more or less successful than other people, we have to define what we mean by success. My definition of success is solving the fundamental problems of this country and the world. And one of these problems is racism.

According to this definition, maybe our children are more successful.

And, finally, there is the question of expectations. Asian American children are successful because their parents expect them to be. Most successful Americans have encountered someone in their lives—a parent, teacher, coach, Big Brother, etc., who has had faith in their ability. My wife always talks favorably of the Catholic high school teacher who believed she could become a writer.

One of the cruelest hoaxes being played on Black children today is the Black peer pressure against academically inclined Black children, accusing them of trying to be White (some of these kids have even been beaten up). Other minority children must handle equally restrictive expectations, both from their own group and from Whites. White kids are often told they can't dance, play certain music, or compete at certain sports.

A biracial child can ignore all these limiting expectations. A biracial child can be what he/she wants to be.

And that's my idea of success!

Organizations to Contact

The editors have compiled the following list of organizations concerned with the issues debated in this book. The descriptions are derived from materials provided by the organizations. All have publications or information available for interested readers. The list was compiled on the date of publication of the present volume; the information provided here may change. Be aware that many organizations take several weeks or longer to respond to inquiries, so allow as much time as possible.

American Civil Liberties Union (ACLU)
125 Broad St., 18th Floor, New York, NY 10004-2400
(212) 549-2500
e-mail: aclu@aclu.org • website: http://www.aclu.org

The ACLU is a national organization that works to defend Americans' civil rights as guaranteed by the U.S. Constitution. It provides legal defense, research, and education. The ACLU publishes and distributes policy statements, pamphlets, and the semiannual newsletter *Civil Liberties Alert.*

Center for the Study of Biracial Children
2300 S. Krameria St., Denver, CO 80222
(303) 692-9008
e-mail: francis@csbc.cncfamily.com
website: http://www.csbc.cncfamily.com

The Center for the Study of Biracial Children produces and disseminates materials for and about interracial families and biracial children. The center provides advocacy, training, and consulting. *Tomorrow's Children,* a book written by Dr. Francis Wardle, one of the foremost authorities on multiethnic identity, can be ordered at the center's website.

Center for the Study of White American Culture
245 W. 4th Ave., Roselle, NJ 07203
(908) 241-5439
e-mail: contact@euroamerican.org • website: http://www.euroamerican.org

The center is a multiracial organization that supports cultural exploration and self-discovery among white Americans. It also encourages dialogue among all racial and cultural groups concerning the role of white American culture in the larger American society. It publishes the Whiteness Papers series, including "Decentering Whiteness" and "White Men and the Denial of Racism."

4C Cross Cultural Couples & Children
PO Box 8, Plainsboro, NJ 08536
(609) 275-9352
e-mail: tango-sierra@geocities.com
website: http://www.geocities.com/Heartland/Meadows/7936/7936.html

4C is a nonprofit support group committed to helping cross-cultural couples as well as children and adults of mixed racial backgrounds. The organization promotes public acceptance of interracial couples and mixed-race individuals, studies problems unique to interracial relationships, and aids in the development of self-esteem in mixed-race individuals. It publishes the quarterly newsletter *Happenings*.

HateWatch
PO Box 380151, Cambridge, MA 02238-0151
(617) 876-3796
e-mail: info@hatewatch.org • website: http://www.hatewatch.org

HateWatch is a web-based organization that monitors hate group activity on the Internet. Its website features information on hate groups and civil rights organizations and their activities. The text of interviews with David Duke and KKK Grand Dragon Paul Deputy are available on HateWatch's website.

Interracial Family Circle (IFC)
PO Box 53291, Washington, DC 20009
(800) 500-9040 • (202) 393-7866
e-mail: ifcweb@hotmail.com
website: http://www.geocities.com/heartland/estates/4496

The Interracial Family Circle strives to protect and advance the rights of interracial/multicultural individuals and families through educational programs. It provides support and community for its members by offering social events. *The Collage*, IFC's newsletter, and a recommended reading list of multiethnic books are available at its website.

Multicultural Council of Saskatchewan (MCoS)
369 Park St., Regina, SK S4N 5B2 CANADA
(306) 721-2767 • fax: (306) 721-3342
e-mail: wluzny@unibase.unibase.com

The Multicultural Council of Saskatchewan promotes positive cross-cultural relations and the recognition of cultural diversity. Its publications include the monthly newsletter *News Circular*, and the magazines *Saskatchewan Multicultural Magazine* and *Our Multicultural Wish*.

National Alliance
PO Box 90, Hillsboro, WV 24946
(304) 653-4600
e-mail: national@natvan.com • website: http://www.natvan.com

The National Alliance is an organization dedicated to the long-term interests of white Americans and to those of European descent around the world. It publishes the monthly newsletter *Free Speech*, the magazine *National Vanguard*, and several leaflets.

National Association for the Advancement of White People (NAAWP)
PO Box 1727, Callahan, FL 32011
(904) 766-2253 • (813) 274-4988 • fax: (904) 924-0716
e-mail: naawp1@mediaone.net • website: http://www.naawp.org

NAAWP is a nonviolent, civil rights organization for white rights. It perceives Caucasians as being discriminated against in favor of special interest minority groups. The association, which seeks to preserve a white heritage, discourages interracial relationships. *NAAWP News* newsletter is published 8–10 times per year.

National Urban League
120 Wall St., New York, NY 10005
(212) 558-5600
e-mail: info@nul.org • website: http://www.nul.org

A community service agency, the National Urban League aims to eliminate institutional racism in the United States. It also provides services for minorities who experience discrimination in employment, housing, welfare, and other areas. Its publications include the books *Marrying the Natives: Love and Interracial Marriage* and *Mixed Matches: How to Create Successful Interracial, Interethnic, and Interfaith Relationships.*

Sojourners
2401 15th St. NW, Washington, DC 20009
(202) 328-8842 • (800) 714-7474 • fax: (202) 328-8757
e-mail: sojourners@sojourners.com • website: http://www.sojourners.com

Sojourners is an ecumenical Christian organization committed to racial justice and reconciliation between races. It publishes *America's Original Sin: A Study Guide on White Racism* as well as the monthly *Sojourners* magazine.

Stormfront
PO Box 6637, West Palm Beach, FL 33405
(561) 833-0030 • fax: (561) 820-0051
e-mail: comments@stormfront.org • website: http://www.stormfront.org

This organization promotes white superiority and serves as a resource for white political and social action groups. Stormfront is intolerant of interracial relationships. It publishes the weekly newsletter *Stormwatch*, and its website contains articles and position papers.

United States Commission on Civil Rights
1121 Vermont Ave. NW, Washington, DC 20425
(202) 376-8177
e-mail: wwwadmin@usccr.gov • website: http://www.usccr.gov

A fact-finding body, the United States Commission on Civil Rights reports directly to Congress and the president on the effectiveness of equal opportunity programs and laws. A catalog of its numerous publications can be obtained from its website.

Bibliography

Books

J. Lawrence Driskill — *Cross-Cultural Marriages and the Church: Living the Global Neighborhood.* Carroll Stream, IL: Hope, 1995.

Martha Hodes, ed. — *Sex, Love, Race: Crossing Boundaries in North American History.* New York: New York University Press, 1999.

Jane Lazarre — *Beyond the Whiteness of Whiteness: Memoir of a White Mother of Black Sons.* Durham, NC: Duke University Press, 1996.

Kevin Luttery and Tonya Martin, eds. — *A Stranger in My Bed.* South Orange, NJ: Bryant & Dillon, 1997.

Robert P. McNamara, Maria Tempenis, and Beth Walton — *Crossing the Line.* Westport, CT: Greenwood, 1999.

Scott Minerbrook — *Divided to the Vein: A Journey into Race and Family.* Orlando, FL: Harcourt Brace, 1996.

Renea D. Nash — *Coping with Interracial Dating.* New York: Rosen, 1997.

Maria P.P. Root, ed. — *The Multiracial Experience: Racial Borders as the New Frontier.* Newbury Park, CA: Sage, 1996.

Joel Williamson — *New People: Miscegenation and Mulattoes in the United States.* Baton Rouge: Louisiana State University Press, 1995.

Robert J.C. Young — *Colonial Desire: Hybridity in Theory, Culture, and Race.* New York: Routledge, 1995.

Periodicals

Jacqueline Adams — "The White Wife," *New York Times Magazine*, September 18, 1994.

Erin Burnette — "The Strengths of Mixed-Race Relationships," *APA Monitor,* September 1995.

Peter Feuerherd — "A New American Tribe: Intermarriage and the Racial Divide," *Commonweal*, September 12, 1997.

Michael A. Fletcher — "Interracial Marriages Eroding Barriers," *Washington Post,* December 28, 1998.

Gloria Wade Gayles — "Brother Pain: How a Black Woman Came to Terms with Interracial Love," *Utne Reader,* November/December 1996.

Lawrence Otis Graham — "Why I Never Dated a White Woman," *Glamour,* June 1995.

Kravitz, Lenny, 67

Latinos, 61
Liu, Eric, 22
Llaga, Kate, 52
London, Scott, 25
Lorde, Audre, 57
Loving, Richard, 7
Loving v. Virginia, 7

Mahon, Patrick, 51
Majete, Clayton, 9
Malcolm X, 6
Marshall, Brian, 18
Maryland, 6, 7
Massachusetts, 6
McMillan, Angela, 49
media, 32, 34, 51
Meridian (Walker), 56
Mexicans, 26
Microsoft Encarta Electronic Encyclopedia, 40
Millard, H., 8
Mills, Candace, 30
miscegenation. *See* interracial marriages
Mod Squad (television show), 54
Moshell, Charlie, 52
Moshell, John, 52
multiculturalism
  demands white genocide, 33
  needs unity/uniqueness approach, 27
  UN vision of, 35
  will produce racial strife, 37–38
multiracial people. *See* biracial adults;
  biracial children
Mystery of the Ages, The (Armstrong), 40, 43, 45

Nakashima, Cynthia, 70, 71
Native Americans, 68
  interracial marriages of, 7
  pollute the white gene pool, 6
  statistical extermination of, 26
New American Standard, 44
North American Free Trade Agreement (NAFTA), 38
North Carolina, 6

O'Brien, Dan, 67
Okina, Betty, 67

Pennsylvania, 6
Perkins, Mitali, 8
Peterson, Karen S., 48
Pitts, Helen, 6
Pocahontas (film), 51
Podhoretz, Norman, 23
Poitier, Sidney, 54
Population Reference Bureau, 30, 31

Poussaint, Alvin, 67

Qian, Zhenchao, 52

Racially Mixed People in America (Wilson), 68, 70
racism, 47
  affects biracial children, 15, 16–17, 69–70, 71
  affects religious policies, 39–40, 45, 46–47
  antimiscegenation laws as, 6–7, 9, 26
  black women's experience of, 56–57
  color hierarchy in, 51
  in concept of hybrid vigor, 70–71
  and interracial marriages, 8, 22–24
  is ignorance, 20, 21, 23
  is not just a black/white issue, 26, 61, 65
  labels people, 14–16, 65
religious groups
  oppose interfaith marriages, 26, 41–42, 43
  racism of, 39–40, 45, 46–47
  support interracial marriages, 32
Rodriguez, Richard, 26
Rosado, Lydia, 51

Sade, 67
Samoans, 26
Shinagawa, Larry Hajime, 51, 52
slavery, 6, 47
Smith's Bible Dictionary, 40
social system. *See* American culture
South Carolina, 6
Streetwise (Anderson), 48
Strom, Kevin Alfred, 28
Supreme Court, 6, 7, 9, 47

Taney, Roger B., 47
teenagers, 7, 48–49, 71
  see also biracial children; interracial dating
Theological Wordbook of the Old Testament, 40
Thompson, Daley, 67
Time magazine, 25
Turlington, Christy, 67

United Nations, 35
Untachantr, Eddie, 49, 51
USA Today/Gallup Poll, 48, 49
U.S. Congress, 6
U.S. Supreme Court, 6, 7, 9, 47

Virginia, 6

Wade, Brenda, 51
Wade-Gayles, Gloria, 54